PRAISE FOR THE OUTLAW SEA

"[Langewiesche's] nail-biting description is more gripping than *The Perfect Storm* or *Titanic*."
—Brad Knickerbocker, *The Christian Science Monitor*

"Langewiesche has evolved into perhaps our leading forensic journalist, a voracious student of all that can go wrong. Like a literary-minded accident investigator, he digs for every shred of evidence, without worrying about whom his conclusions might offend." —Bill Gifford, *The Washington Post Book World*

"An ambitious and lyrical evocation of the role the oceans play in an increasingly interconnected planet . . . Elegant."
—*New York Post* ("Required Reading")

"In understated prose that highlights the dangers inherent in the freedom of the seas, Mr. Langewiesche points out the helplessness of American officials who believe that a large-scale maritime terrorist attack currently poses the most serious threat to their national security . . . Mr. Langewiesche is especially good on how the ocean, which 'looks tight in print,' can descend into such chaos in practice." —*The Economist*

"Punctuated with harrowing scenes of shipwrecks, oil spills and pirate attacks, *The Outlaw Sea* is impossible to put down."
—Alex Abramovich, *People*

"William Langewiesche is that rare magazine writer whose narrative journalism has a shelf life longer than a week or a month . . . A magisterial effort of reporting." —Philip Connors, *Newsday*

"Langewiesche's prose is always elegant and gripping for its restraint. But there is another pleasure in reading him: the plea-

Sam Parsons

WILLIAM LANGEWIESCHE
THE OUTLAW SEA

WILLIAM LANGEWIESCHE is the author of four previous books, *Cutting for Sign*, *Sahara Unveiled*, *Inside the Sky*, and *American Ground*. He is a national correspondent for *The Atlantic Monthly*, where this book originated.

Also by William Langewiesche

Cutting for Sign

Sahara Unveiled

Inside the Sky

American Ground

THE OUTLAW SEA

THE OUTLAW SEA

A World of Freedom, Chaos, and Crime

WILLIAM LANGEWIESCHE

North Point Press

A division of Farrar, Straus and Giroux

New York

North Point Press
A division of Farrar, Straus and Giroux
18 West 18th Street, New York 10011

Published in 2004 by North Point Press
First paperback edition, 2005

Grateful acknowledgment is made to *The Atlantic Monthly*, where portions of
this book originated.

The Library of Congress has cataloged the hardcover edition as follows:
Langewiesche, William.
    The outlaw sea : a world of freedom, chaos, and crime /
William Langewiesche.—1st ed.
        p. cm.
    ISBN 0-86547-581-4 (hardcover : alk. paper)
    1. Shipping. 2. Merchant marine. 3. Terrorism. 4. Ships—Nationality.
5. Law of the sea. 6. Seafaring life. I. Title.

HE571.L36   2004
387.5'44—dc22   2003028112

Paperback ISBN-13: 978-0-86547-722-3
Paperback ISBN-10: 0-86547-722-1

Designed by Jonathan D. Lippincott
Maps designed by Jeffrey L. Ward

www.fsgbooks.com

To sailors at sea

CONTENTS

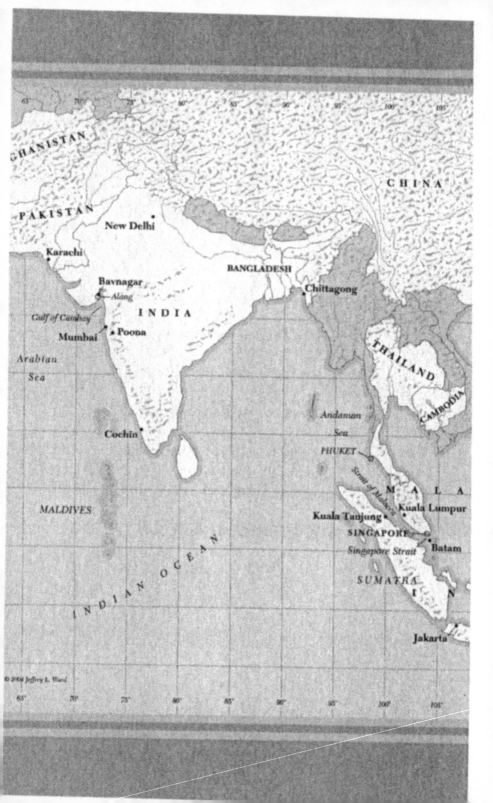

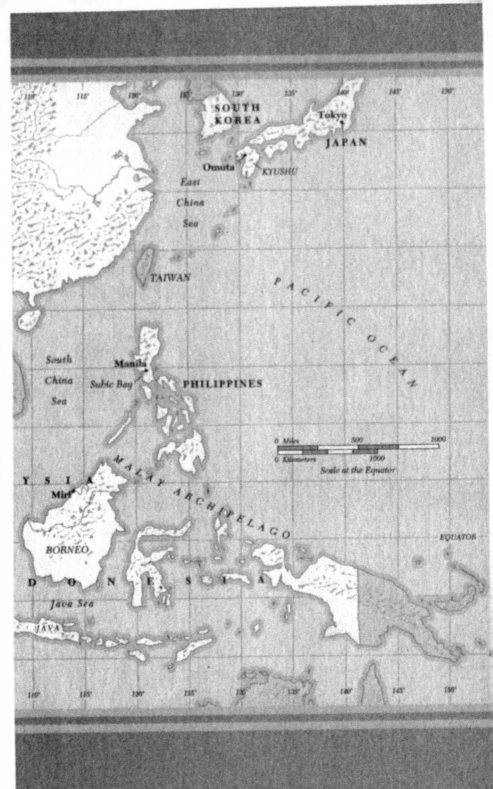

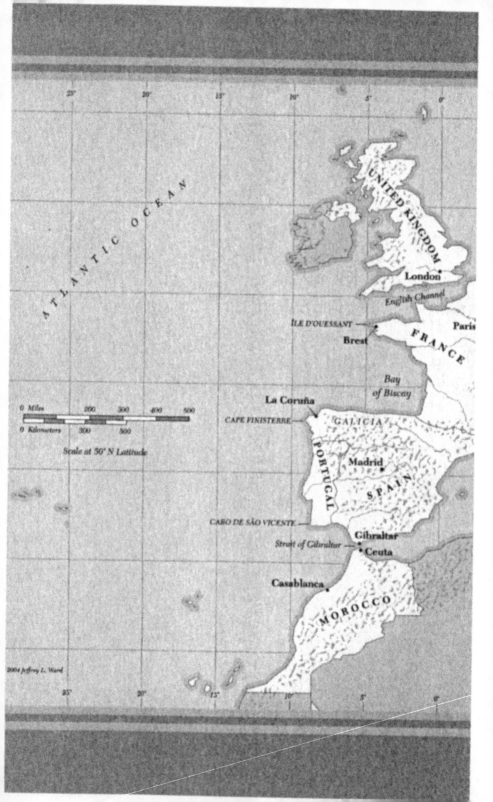

THE OUTLAW SEA

AN OCEAN WORLD

Since we live on land, and are usually beyond sight of the sea, it is easy to forget that our world is an ocean world, and to ignore what in practice that means. Some shores have been tamed, however temporarily, but beyond the horizon lies a place that refuses to submit. It is the wave maker, an anarchic expanse, the open ocean of the high seas. Under its many names, and with variations in color and mood, this single ocean spreads across three-fourths of the globe. Geographically, it is not the exception to our planet, but by far its greatest defining feature. By political and social measures it is important too—not merely as a wilderness that has always existed or as a reminder of the world as it was before, but also quite possibly as a harbinger of a larger chaos to come. That is neither a lament nor a cheap forecast of doom, but more simply an observation of modern life in a place that is rarely seen. At a time when every last patch of land is claimed by one government or another, and when citizenship is treated as an absolute condition of human existence, the ocean is a realm that remains radically free.

Expressing that freedom are more than forty thousand large merchant ships that wander the world with little or no regulation, plying the open ocean among uncountable numbers of smaller coastal craft and carrying nearly the full weight of international trade—almost all the raw materials and finished products on which our land lives are built. The ships are steel behemoths, slow and enormously efficient, and magnificent if only for their mass and functionality. They are crewed from pools of the poor—several million sailors of varying quality, largely now from southern Asia, who bid down for the jobs in a global market and are mixed together without reference to such petty conventions as language and nationality. The sailors do not enjoy the benefit of long stays in exotic ports, as sailors did until recently, but rather they live afloat for twelve months at a stretch, enduring a maritime limbo in the ships' fluorescent-lit quarters, making brief stops to load and unload, and rarely going ashore. They are employed by independent Third World "manning agents," who in turn are paid for the labor they provide by furtive offshore management companies that in many cases work for even more elusive owners—people whose identities are hidden behind the legal structures of corporations so ghostly and unencumbered that they exist only on paper, or maybe as a brass plate on some faraway foreign door. The purpose of such arrangements is not to make philosophical points about the rule of law, but to limit responsibility, maximize profits, and allow for total freedom of action in a highly competitive world. The ships themselves are expressions of this system as it has evolved. They are possibly the most independent objects on earth, many of them without allegiances of any kind, frequently changing their identity and assuming whatever nationality—or "flag"—allows them to proceed as they please.

This is the starting point of understanding the freedom of the sea. No one pretends that a ship must come from the home port painted on its stern, or that it has ever been anywhere near. Panama is the largest maritime nation on earth, followed by bloody Liberia, which hardly exists. No coastline is required either. There are ships that hail from La Paz, in landlocked Bolivia. There are ships that hail from the Mongolian desert. Moreover, the registries themselves are rarely based in the countries whose names they carry: Panama is considered to be an old-fashioned "flag" because its consulates handle the paperwork and collect the registration fees, but "Liberia" is run by a company in Virginia, "Cambodia" by another in South Korea, and the proud and independent "Bahamas" by a group in the City of London.

The system in its modern form, generally known as "flags of convenience," began in the early days of World War II as an American invention sanctioned by the United States government to circumvent its own neutrality laws. The idea was to allow American-owned ships to be re-flagged as Panamanian and used to deliver materials to Britain without concern that their action (or loss) would drag the United States unintentionally into war. Afterward, of course, the United States did join the war—only to emerge several years later with the largest ship registry in the world. By then the purely economic benefits of the Panamanian arrangement had become clear: it would allow the industry to escape the high costs of hiring American crews, to reduce the burdens imposed by stringent regulation, to limit the financial consequences of the occasional foundering or loss of a ship. And so an exodus occurred. For the same reasons, a group of American oil companies subsequently created the Liberian registry (based at first in New York) for their tankers, as a "development" or international aid project. Again the scheme was sanctioned by the U.S. government, this time by idealists at the Department of State. For several decades these two quasi-colonial registries, which attracted shipowners from around the world, maintained reasonably high technical standards, perhaps because behind the scenes they were still subject to some control by the "gentlemen's club" of traditional maritime powers—principally Europe and the United States. In the 1980s, however, a slew of other countries woke up to the potential for revenues and began to create their own registries to compete for business. The result was a sudden expansion in flags of convenience, and a corresponding loss of control. This happened in the context of an increasingly strong internationalist democratic ideal, by which all countries were formally considered to be equal. The trend accelerated in the 1990s, and paradoxically in direct reaction to a United Nations effort to impose order by demanding a "genuine link" between a ship and its flag—a vague requirement that, typically, was subverted by the righteous "compliance" of everyone involved.

These developments were seemingly as organic as they were calculated or man-made. For the shipowners, they amounted to a profound liberation. By shopping globally, they found that they could choose the laws that were applied to them, rather than haplessly submitting to the jurisdictions of their native countries. The advantages were so great that even the most conservative and well-established shipowners, who were perhaps not naturally inclined to abandon the confines of the nation-state, found that they had no choice but to do so. What's more, because of the registration fees the shipowners could offer to cash-strapped governments and corrupt officials, the various flags competed for business, and the deals kept getting better.

The resulting arrangement, though deeply subversive, has an undeniably elegant design. It constitutes an exact reversal of sovereignty's intent and a perfect mockery of national conceits. It is free enterprise at its freest, a logic taken to extremes. And it is by no means always a bad thing. I've been told, for example, that the cost of transporting tea to England has fallen a hundredfold since the days of sail, and even more in recent years. There are similar efficiencies across the board. But the efficiencies are accompanied by global problems too, including the playing of the poor against the poor and the persistence of huge fleets of dangerous ships, the pollution they cause, the implicit disposability of their crews, and the parallel growth of two particularly resilient pathogens that exist now on the ocean—the first being a modern strain of piracy, and the second its politicized cousin, the maritime form of the new, stateless terrorism. The patterns are strong in part because they fit so well with the long-standing realities of the sea—the ocean's easy disregard for human constructs, its size, the strength of its storms, and the privacy provided by its horizons. Certainly the old maritime traditions of freedom are involved, but something new is happening too. It is not by chance that the more sophisticated pirate groups and terrorists seem to mimic the methods and operational techniques of the shipowners. Their morals and motivations are different, of course, but all have learned to work without the need for a home base and, more significantly, to escape the forces of order not by running away, but by complying with the laws and regulations in order to move about freely and to hide in plain sight.

The result has been to place the oceans increasingly beyond governmental control. To maritime and security officials in administrative capitals like London and Washington, D.C., steeped in their own traditions of national power, these developments have come in recent years as a surprise. For public consumption, the officials still talk bravely about the impact of new regulations and the promise of technology, but in private many admit that it is chaos, not control, that is on the rise. They have learned what future historians may be able to see even more clearly, that our world is an ocean world, and it is wild.

The *Kristal* was therefore a typical casualty of modern times. It was an all-purpose tanker, 560 feet long, that had been built in Italy in 1974 and for more than a quarter century had restlessly wandered the world, riding the downward spiral of the maritime market under a progression of names, owners, and nationalities. By the winter of 2001, at the advanced age of twenty-seven, it was flying the flag of Malta—a registry of convenience, with a typically shoddy track record and a reputation for allowing owners to operate their vessels nearly as they pleased. The ship belonged to an obscure but law-abiding Italian family whose members had an understandable penchant for privacy. They owned it through the device of a Maltese holding company that existed only on paper, as a mailing address in the capital, Valletta, the home port painted on the ship's stern. There is no evidence that the *Kristal* ever stopped there, though it did sometimes sail through the Mediterranean and so must occasionally have passed by. It was crewed by manning agents primarily in Karachi, Pakistan, but also in Spain and Croatia. Its business and maintenance were managed through layers of other companies, variously of Switzerland and Monaco.

Though the *Kristal* was well painted and regularly passed inspections, it was at least five years beyond the ideal retirement age, and had grown decrepit and difficult to maintain. Its owners kept it sailing anyway, apparently with the intention of squeezing a final few years of profitability from the hull before selling it to other operators still lower on the food chain or, if none could be found, directly to a shipbreaker for the scrap value of its steel. They were unable to attract business from the major oil companies, most of which now try to apply stringent standards to the tankers they charter and generally shy away from vessels past the age of twenty because of the risk of breakup, and the expense and negative publicity caused by spills. Nonetheless, there were plenty of other, less exacting customers available, as long as the *Kristal* could transport their cargoes at a low enough price. Indeed, the *Kristal* was constantly busy. Throughout the previous year, it had engaged in a regular globe-circling trade, carrying molasses from India to western Europe, kerosene from Latvia to Argentina, and soy oil from Argentina around Cape Horn to India again. The molasses was a sign of the *Kristal's* decline: it is the product left over from refined sugar, a low-value cargo carried on the cheap by ships that are typically one step removed from the grave. There is little risk to the principals involved—the customers and shipping companies—because the hulls and cargoes are insured, and in the event of an accident and a spill, molasses disperses easily and disappears without a trace. It is no small matter in choosing a ship that the same is generally true of Third World crews.

The *Kristal's* customer in February 2001 was a subsidiary of the big British sugar company Tate & Lyle, which had contracted with the ship's owners to bring a full, heavy load of twenty-eight thousand tons of molasses from two ports on the west coast of India to an unspecified European destination that would be decided en route on the basis of the market. The crew consisted of thirty-five men of various nationalities, mostly Pakistani—about ten men more than usual for a ship of this type, because they would need to carry out repairs while under way. Such repairs are standard in the industry, and have the double advantage of allowing ships to avoid both costly layups and the prying eyes of inspectors. Aboard the *Kristal* most of the repairs consisted of chipping with hammers and chisels at heavy rust that had spread like a cancer under the paint, across the main deck and through the hull. There have been reports, difficult to substantiate but entirely plausible, that considerable and illicit welding was also being performed, and that as a result, one of the cargo tanks could not be used—a restriction that may have caused the crew to load the molasses improperly, placing severe strains on the ship's structure. It seems unlikely that this could have occurred without at least the tacit approval of the ship's management company. Be that as it may, the crew certainly knew about the *Kristal*'s precarious condition and were glad for their jobs nonetheless.

The captain was a forty-three-year-old Croatian named Allen Marin—one of many such officers from former Communist states, who are known to be competent and able to live on low salaries and who now constitute something of a global officer caste at service on increasing numbers of ships. Marin was an affable character, and he was well liked by his subordinates aboard, though some of them thought that he seemed strangely uninterested in the technical aspects of running the ship. It was noticed, for instance, that during the important final loading of the molasses in India, he and the chief mate, another Croatian, went ashore overnight, leaving supervision of the work to a junior officer. No one objected, of course. The *Kristal* was a molasses ship, but a fairly happy one. The attitude was to let the captain have his fun.

On February 4, 2001, the *Kristal* set out across the Indian Ocean on a route that would take it through the Suez Canal and the Strait of Gibraltar. The days passed in monotonous succession, broken by the routine of alternating six-hour watches, the anticipation of work and of rest. During their time off, the men ate and slept, and they relaxed by playing Ping-Pong or watching films in the messrooms. There were three such messrooms: one for the officers and cadets, who were both Croatian and Pakistani; one for the skilled sailors, who included three Spaniards; and one for the remainder of the crew, the ordinary hands, all of whom were Pakistani. The Pakistanis were fed a native cuisine of spicy foods that conformed to Islamic restrictions. They liked to watch Indian films, full of weddings and dancing. The others preferred the slicker Hollywood fare, with sleek women and guns. The two groups knew each other well, and they mixed, but they were not necessarily pals. They called the superstructure where they lived the "iron house," because it was made of metal and hemmed them in. It stood aft on the hull and rose five levels above the main deck to the bridge. It was not uncomfortable, but after a while it seemed small. The crew's conversations there were almost exclusively about the ship, because after many months together it provided all that was left to be said.

The Indian Ocean was calm. Word came that the destination would be Amsterdam. There was a period of concern partway to the Red Sea, when a portion of the main deck suddenly bulged upward, breaking some welds. Captain Marin reported the problem to the management company and received a private reply, presumably to carry on. Only one crewman expressed grave concern. He was one of the three Spaniards, a bearish, bearded forty-one-year-old pumpman named Juan Carlos Infante Casas, who despite his enormous physical strength had a reputation as a worrier. Infante Casas's duties included operating the valves and cargo pumps and sounding the tanks from overhead on the deck. Like the other Spaniards, both of whom were mechanics, he came from Galicia, along La Costa del Morte, Spain's western Atlantic shore. He had gone to sea out of restlessness as a young man, and had never married, and still lived with his mother, to whom he was close. The sailor's life was not the adventure he had hoped it would be, but he had stayed with it for lack of choice, and for nearly two decades he endured the steady loss of income and security experienced first by Europeans and Americans and then by all the successive rearguards of whatever nationality on the increasingly anarchic seas. After six months aboard, he was looking forward to leaving the ship just a few days ahead, at a scheduled fueling stop and partial crew change in Gibraltar. In messroom conversation he said that he knew the *Kristal* too well to trust it on the winter Atlantic. The other Spaniards felt more equable, though they too were scheduled to leave at Gibraltar. The older of them was a lean, graying man, nearly sixty, named José Manuel Castineiras, who said that he neither regretted nor enjoyed his life at sea but considered it his destiny. It was easier for him than for his friend Infante Casas, therefore, when, after the *Kristal* passed through the Suez Canal, word came that the Gibraltar stop had been eliminated: the ship would fuel instead at Ceuta, on the Moroccan side of the strait, and the crew change would be delayed until Amsterdam. That too was destiny.

The passage through the Mediterranean was uneventful. To keep to schedule, Captain Marin maintained the full engine speed of 88 rpm, driving the heavy ship westward at 11 knots through six-foot waves that were typically steep for that sea. The hull shuddered sometimes, but the ship barely pitched, and it rolled side to side by only 5 degrees—not enough even to spill coffee. Spray wet the forward deck. The crew chipped rust. Life in the iron house continued normally.

The *Kristal* arrived at Ceuta on February 24. A storm was forecast for the Atlantic ahead, along the Portuguese and Spanish coasts, and gale warnings were in effect farther to the north. Marin ordered four hundred tons of bunker fuel, enough for another twelve days. While the ship took on the fuel, Juan Carlos Infante Casas went ashore and called his mother, who doted on him. When she answered the phone, he said, *"Hola Española,"* which is what he always said. He told her that he was calling from Ceuta and that his return to Galicia had been delayed.

His mother said, "We have arranged your room."

Infante Casas said, "Please don't make special arrangements."

She said, "Why? What do you mean?"

He said, "The ship is in very bad condition." He told her its name, which until then she had not known. He asked about the weather in Galicia. She reported that it was very nice.

But her view was limited, as land views are, by the orderly little neighborhood that surrounded her and the sky immediately overhead. At most, she might have seen on television a simplified prediction that tomorrow the sun would hide behind clouds. While fueling in Ceuta, Captain Marin had access to more sophisticated forecasts, as well as to reports of troubles ahead: ships were reporting heavy seas off the coasts of Portugal and Spain and to the north toward England across the notorious Bay of Biscay. In earlier, more orderly times he might have been expected to go gently on his aging ship, and to wait in port until the weather had passed. But on the free-market sea, where profit margins are slim, delays of even a few hours can seem unacceptably costly, and a captain who develops a reputation for timidity will soon find that someone has taken his place. As soon as the fueling was finished, therefore, Captain Marin ordered the ship to get under way, and in the last

hours before midnight of February 24 he sent the *Kristal* sailing
fast past the Rock of Gibraltar and on into the Atlantic night.

At once the ride grew rough. The waves at first were about
twelve feet high—black swells more felt than seen, across
which the *Kristal* pitched and rolled and occasionally bashed.
Such conditions were not in themselves immediately worrisome:
the local winds remained light, and in technical terms the sea state
seemed to be only about Force 5, on a scale of twelve. Nonetheless, the swells were evidence of a significant disturbance ahead,
the barometer was falling, and it was clear that worse was to come.
With a schedule to keep, Captain Marin maintained full engine
speed. The weather's resistance slowed the ship by about 2 knots
as it fought northwestward to round the Cabo de São Vicente, on
the Portuguese coast.

At 2:00 a.m. a twenty-five-year-old Pakistani deck cadet
named Naeem Uddin joined the officers on the bridge to begin
his regular six-hour watch. Uddin was a tall, docile man who had
grown up in northern Pakistan, on the border with China, as the
son of a security guard. Under the mistaken impression that the
merchant marine would provide some of the discipline and pride
of a naval career, he had trained to become a deck officer at an
academy in Karachi. After three years aboard working ships, he
knew better now, but with debts piled up behind him and only
three months of required sea time remaining before he would
qualify for his first license, he felt committed to the life. To make
the best of it, he provided the discipline for himself, working hard
without complaint and never commenting on the wisdom of his

superiors. He was not, however, without judgment. When Uddin came onto the bridge, the second officer, whose watch it was, told him that the autopilot was being overwhelmed and that he should take the helm and steer. This was one of Uddin's standard duties, and he performed it well, carefully holding the headings as commanded, but not without wondering, as the hours went by, whether there wasn't some better way to handle the coming storm than busting straight through.

Two years before, while serving aboard an Iranian freighter, Uddin had witnessed an argument between a chief mate and captain about just such a question. They were on a trip from India to the Persian Gulf, with a typhoon ahead. The chief mate had recommended taking a circuitous route along the coast to avoid the worst of the storm, but the captain, worried about the additional eight hours that such a tactic would cost, had said, "Whatever happens, we're going straight." As a result, they were caught by winds and waves so great that the ship's engine was overpowered, and with rpm set for "full ahead," they found themselves dead in the water, sometimes even moving backward. Since the rudder was ineffective at less than about 5 knots, they lost the ability to steer, and for twenty-four hours they drifted helplessly until the storm abated. It was merely by luck that they had sufficient sea room and did not end up wrecked against a lee shore. This time, as Uddin knew, the sea room was more limited: the land was out of sight, but should the *Kristal* turn or drift to the right, it would soon encounter breakers on the Iberian shores.

Steadily over the next two days the weather grew worse. The *Kristal* struggled northward in the open ocean off the Portuguese coast, headed for a point abeam Spain's Cape Finisterre, where it would be able to turn slightly eastward and take a straight line across the outer Bay of Biscay for the famously stormy French island of Ouessant, which stands at the southern entrance to the English Channel. By now the sea was so rough that all work on the deck had stopped. Sleep was difficult, movie watching nauseating, Ping-Pong a dangerous sport. Ships coming from the north warned of still rougher stuff ahead. Captain Marin seemed detached as usual. He maintained full forward speed.

By late afternoon on February 26, on the second day after passing Gibraltar, the *Kristal* was offshore of Galicia, in the vicinity of Cape Finisterre, and conditions by any standard were severe. The sea state by now was at least Force 9. To the men on the bridge, the ocean seemed to be coming apart. The wind howled out of the north, above a constant roar of crashing water. Sheets of heavy spray rose to smash against the bridge's wings. The waves were steep and breaking, as high as thirty feet. They regularly buried the bow and sometimes swept across the entire deck, engulfing the ship to the superstructure and filling the aft passageways faster than they could drain.

The view from a ship of such conditions is in some ways a privileged one—a rare display of the ocean's power that may seem exhilarating even to a crew fighting for survival. There is for instance a home video of a violent storm in the Mediterranean off Spain that was shot in December 2000 from the bridge of a Greek-owned gasoline tanker named the *Castor*, in which waves are seen burying the deck, and in the background the Polish crew can be heard laughing and whooping with delight. That crew proved foolish, because the *Castor* then cracked severely and, threatening at any moment to sink or explode, embarked on what became an epic voyage under tow as a "leper ship" that for six weeks was refused entry by every port of refuge. Nonetheless, there is no denying the abstract beauty of a heavy storm at sea.

But the crew of the *Kristal* knew their ship too well to indulge in abstraction. At 2:00 a.m., when Naeem Uddin entered the bridge for his watch, he found not only the scheduled second officer on duty there but the chief mate and the third officer as well, both of whom had stayed on past the end of their normal watches. To Uddin they looked afraid, as was he. The blackness of the night was streaked with the white of breaking waves. The ship was rolling and pitching violently. Through the spinning clear-screens on the bridge's windows he could see the familiar bow light moving wildly as the ship plunged into the oncoming waves. It was just possible to make out the masses of water boiling across the deck. When Uddin took the helm, he found the ship difficult to steer. It was hogging over the crests, surfing down the watery slopes, sagging and staggering through the troughs, and slewing left and right by 20 degrees. There was no chance of keeping the *Kristal* exactly on heading. Uddin fought back with large rudder movements, trying to average the swings.

It was not Uddin's first experience with the *Kristal* in a storm. The previous winter, he had steered through similar waves while bound for Ireland with another load of molasses, and he had watched the ship rolling to 25 degrees, uncomfortably close to its capsize threshold. On that occasion, however, the captain had been another man, a Spaniard, who had ordered Uddin to turn the *Kristal* into the waves and slow it to its minimum maneuvering speed, easing the ship's motion at the cost of a delay. This time, in contrast, Captain Marin was below in his cabin, probably asleep. He had stood duty on the bridge for much of the time since leaving Ceuta, and undoubtedly he needed to rest.

Meanwhile, the helm's instrumentation showed that the engine power was still set at the full 88 rpm—as if before retiring, the captain had given an order to maintain the maximum possible speed at all costs.

Uddin was very aware of his low rank as a cadet, and he continued to steer without comment, but he sensed that this ride was more dangerous than any he had known before. Though the *Kristal* was rolling less steeply than it had during the previous year's storm, initially to only about 15 degrees, it was shaking, slamming, and pitching severely through the waves. From the changes in vibration it seemed that the propeller at times was either cavitating or coming partially out of the water. In combination the motions were complex. The ship would roll three or four times, bury its bow, and, while struggling upward, oscillate more rapidly. Uddin realized that enormous strains were being placed on a weak and rusty hull.

The officers on the bridge realized it too. They were openly anxious about the ship's fate, and they repeatedly asked one another, "What's going to happen? What should we do?" The second officer radioed to another vessel that was out that night, running downwind from the north. He asked about the ocean ahead. The answer came back that it was very, very rough, with really high seas—meaning worse even than these. The chief mate and the second officer discussed running for shelter on the Spanish or Portuguese coast, but perhaps because of the dangers of such lee shores, they did not pursue the idea. On several occasions when the slamming grew most intense, the chief mate asked Uddin to alter the course off-wind, 10 or 20 degrees to the west, but each time, the rolling grew so severe that he hastily remanded the order and had the ship brought back to face the storm. The best compromise seemed to lie among compass headings slightly to the left of the weather, by which the ship took the waves on the starboard bow. It wasn't much of a solution. The *Kristal* continued to pitch and slam, and at the extremes rolled past 25 degrees, making it impossible for the officers to stand without holding on, and causing loose objects in the bridge to slide, topple, and crash. Significantly, the chief mate did not rouse the captain or take it upon himself to break the schedule and reduce the engine speed.

Uddin's watch was shortened that night in recognition of the fight he had put up to maintain control. He went below before dawn, had a cold meal, and retreated to his cabin to rest. His cabin was on the galley deck, three levels below the bridge and two above the main deck, at the front of the superstructure, overlooking the bow. It had a bunk, a cabinet with drawers, and a forward-facing porthole covered by a curtain. Uddin undressed, put on nightclothes, and lay in his bunk as usual with his head toward the bow and his feet toward the stern. By wedging himself against the bunk's preventer board, he managed to sleep.

U ddin woke to a series of severe jerks accompanied by the crash of crockery in the galley and the shouts of men. It was 12:30 in the afternoon. He felt groggy and disoriented, and he assumed that the weather had turned worse—that the ship must simply have rolled more heavily than before. But then he noticed that his feet were higher than his head, and indeed that the entire cabin sloped down steeply, toward the bow. The engine had stopped; there were no vibrations. Uddin heard the splashing of water. He scrambled out of the bunk, went to the porthole, and drew aside the curtain. The scene outside sent a shock of terror

through him: the *Kristal*'s hull had broken nearly in two from below and had folded down at the midpoint into a V that was awash
and flexing, hanging together merely by the skin of the deck. The
ship was dead in the water. Storm waves surged through the
breach.

Though in retrospect there had been plenty of advance warning of the *Kristal*'s vulnerability to such a disaster, it was a confus-
ing moment aboard the ship. As the break occurred, the men on
duty up on the bridge saw a cloud of steam rising from rupturing
pipes on the main deck. Some of the crew later said that despite
the conditions at the time, the Spanish pumpman, Juan Carlos Infante Casas, was moving along a catwalk directly above the break
and that he ran for his life upslope toward the superstructure,
barely keeping ahead of the advancing water as the hull angled
downward into the sea. His friend, the lean, graying mechanic,
José Manuel Castineiras, was in the messroom, finishing a lunch
of chicken and soup, when he felt a shock and heard the ship rup-
ture. It made a sharp, heavy crack like a cannon shot, after which
within seconds the deck pitched down. Castineiras rushed outside
onto a passageway and clambered hand over hand up a stairway to
the deck above, where he and other crewmen broke out life jackets and put them on. The general alarm rang. Without further en-
couragement they began to gather at the assigned muster stations
and prepared to abandon ship.

Later it was pointed out that even mortally wounded tankers
tend to float for a while, that molasses does not burn, and that
there was really no need for the crew to hurry. The old adage was
mentioned that sailors should only step *up* into lifeboats—meaning as a desperate last resort when the hull sinks away below their
feet. In reality, however, things are rarely so clear. This crew was
not sitting in some office thinking back on an event; they were en-

during the chaos of the ocean in present time, clustered on the tilted deck of a broken hull in a ferocious winter storm, facing the prospect of imminent death. The air temperature was 39 degrees, and the water was only slightly warmer. The *Kristal* was equipped with an inflatable life raft in a canister and two open lifeboats on davits, one on each side. Had the stern suddenly sunk, as it seemed about to do, it would have tangled the lines, dragged the lifeboats down, and possibly taken the raft as well. It is regrettable that many of the men panicked, and that in their haste some of those now outside on the deck had not dressed beyond the shorts and T-shirts that they happened to have on. But it is also understandable that they urgently lowered the lifeboats to the level of their deck and began to scramble in.

Captain Marin and the chief mate had been dining in the officers' messroom when the accident occurred, and they quickly climbed to the bridge. As they rushed in, they heard the third engineer, on duty in the subsurface confines of the engine room, repeatedly calling on the intercom for clarification. The engineer was a Serb. All he knew for certain was that the engine had shut down automatically, that the overload alarm had sounded, and that his attempt to restart the equipment had failed. His first concern was the loss of control—and indeed with the bow rearing out of the water and acting as a sail, the broken hull had slewed to the west and was rolling dangerously. Now the fire alarms were going off (perhaps triggered by the steam), and he could make no sense of this at all. Captain Marin was nearly as confused, which may explain why he later reported that he had a fire in the engine room, when in reality he did not. He knew in any case that the ship was lost, and he ordered the third engineer to abandon his efforts immediately and evacuate the engine space. Then he got on the radio and broadcast the first emergency call.

In his cabin, braced against the sloping floor, Naeem Uddin donned a heavy sweater over his nightclothes, put on fresh coveralls and shoes, and strapped himself tightly into a life jacket. Oddly, he heard no alarms. Indeed, he was impressed by the silence of the dying ship—a quiet interrupted only by the crash of falling objects and the rhythmic banging of his cabin door, which had popped open and was swinging with the *Kristal's* rolls. He staggered down the deserted hallway, shouldered through a doorway to the outside, and emerged into the roar of the storm.

By then maybe ten minutes had passed since the catastrophe had struck. Uddin was the last man to arrive at the port-side muster station, which was on the leeward, or downwind, side of the ship. By the time he got there, the port lifeboat was hanging just outboard of the deck, and twenty-two of the crew had already climbed in. The Croatian chief engineer was there, as were all three Spaniards and a large number of ordinary Pakistani sailors. Uddin saw two higher-ranking Pakistanis standing on the deck beside the boat—including the third officer who had been on the bridge the night before and who now held a crew list and was checking off names. That third officer was Kenneth Romal, a Karachi native not quite twenty-eight. He was listening to shouted instructions and reassurances from Captain Marin, who stood two levels higher, on the port bridge wing. The men in the lifeboat were silent, and obviously very afraid. Uddin climbed into the bow of the lifeboat, which because of the ship's angle was pointed slightly down. He noticed that the water below was thick with molasses and that the spilled cargo was calming the waves.

Third Officer Romal had a handheld radio with which he could communicate with Captain Marin. Romal climbed in and sat in the stern of the lifeboat, at the helm. After another ten minutes the captain gave the order to abandon ship; and the chief mate, standing one deck higher, used a brake arrangement to ease the port lifeboat into the waves. Twenty-five men were aboard. They unshackled the boat from the cables, started the small diesel engine, and drifted clear of the ship. From the bridge wing the captain radioed for them to try to hold position close by in case of difficulties as, next, the chief mate lowered the starboard lifeboat, with an additional eight men aboard. The starboard lifeboat was on the ship's upwind side, bearing the full brunt of the storm, and as the captain had expected, it had trouble in the heavy seas: the sailors could not disengage the boat from one of the davit wires, which with every high wave now bowed like a giant snare, threatening to slip under the boat and capsize it. Uddin saw the captain and first mate rushing about the bridge, anxiously monitoring the struggle below. Eventually the starboard lifeboat was freed, but then it began to drift forward along the broken hull toward the breach—a rage of breaking seas that would surely kill the men if they were swept in. Uddin and the others in the port lifeboat watched in frustration, unable to intervene. Somehow the starboard lifeboat moved clear. Carrying its crew of eight frightened sailors, it faded rapidly into the storm and disappeared from view.

Captain Marin and the chief mate were alone now on the ship. Some in the port lifeboat argued for returning to try to pick them up, but the captain insisted by radio that the ship was about to sink, and they should steer clear. It was an extraordinarily brave gesture—a private display of honor by a man who must have known that his own captains ashore, those shadowy companies whose schedules he had so dutifully served, would never have taken such risks for him. For the moment, at least, this did not seem to matter. He and the first mate checked through the entire superstructure for possible stragglers, even going below the waterline to search the engine room. When they were sure that no one had been left behind, they returned to the deck and managed to deploy the inflatable life raft despite the ferocious winds. They then jumped down into it and floated free.

Aboard the port lifeboat, the crew had already lost sight of the *Kristal*. The suddenness with which they found themselves alone was almost as frightening as the facts that faced them. They had no idea of their destination, or even if their plight was known. Third Officer Romal was steering skillfully, but they were twenty-five sailors without survival suits on a bitterly cold ocean, moving among mountainous seas in a small open boat, battered by wind and spray. They veered between roaring breakers, any of which could have rolled or swamped their fragile craft. Sitting at the bow with the masses of water hissing and rearing overhead, Uddin tried and failed to estimate the size of the waves. They were later said to be thirty feet high—a clinical measure that cannot convey the sea's dimensions as perceived by the *Kristal's* terrified castaways, and does not account for the likelihood that several times an hour under such conditions, waves would come along that were nearly twice that high. Romal kept cautioning the men to stay calm, but with limited success. Uddin and several others remained functional. But one man was seasick and vomiting, and many of the others were seized by a dangerously unreasoned animalistic craving to survive. Romal was able to maintain control for a while, but the storm pressed in relentlessly and did not allow his men the space to collect their minds.

It is useful to remember the reductive effect that fear has on thoughts and reactions: whether during shipwrecks or in other disasters, a sort of tunnel vision may set in and narrow people's views. There is another story that comes to mind. It took place three years before the *Kristal*'s demise, on a similarly old and rusty ship named the *Flare*, which had set off from Rotterdam on a stormy winter crossing to Montreal. The *Flare* was a dry-bulk carrier, flagged in Cyprus, carrying a typically multinational crew of twenty-five men. The voyage was extremely rough, with waves exceeding fifty feet. For two weeks the *Flare* slammed and whipped, flexing so wildly that, according to one survivor, the tops of the deck cranes appeared at times to touch. Late one night as it approached the Canadian coast, the *Flare* broke cleanly in two. No one at first was lost. The entire crew clustered on the stern section, which listed to the side and began to sink. Strangely, the engine continued to turn, slowly driving the hulk on an erratic course through the night. The crew managed to launch one lifeboat, but it broke away before anyone could climb aboard. The men were terrified and panicky, and for good reason, since ultimately twenty-one of them died. But before the end, on the sinking stern, there was a moment of savage joy when a ship floating in the opposite direction suddenly loomed out of the darkness ahead, as if it were coming to rescue them. The frightened men cheered—only then to their horror to see the name *Flare* painted in block letters on the side. It was of course their own detached bow section, and it passed them by.

Something similar happened to the crew in the *Kristal*'s port lifeboat. They never saw the *Kristal* again, but at the top of a wave Uddin spotted another ship coming toward them and gave a shout, and the men responded euphorically, with only one idea in mind—the immediate salvation to be found on that ship's deck. Apparently they gave no thought to the difficulty of climbing a ship's sides in such seas, and they never discussed the possibility of waiting for helicopters and rescue divers, which, if they were not already on the way, could quickly now have been brought into play.

Third Officer Romal seemed to be as single-minded as the others: he headed the lifeboat at full speed for the ship while the excited men fired off rocket flares. On the handheld radio Romal began broadcasting, "Mayday! Mayday! This is *Kristal Lifeboat Number One*, with twenty-five men on board!" He repeated this several times until the ship answered.

It took twenty minutes to close the distance.

The rescuer was a Panamanian-flagged gas carrier named the *Tarquin Dell*, with a Filipino captain and crew. Gas carriers are high-sided vessels, and this one was particularly so, with a main deck about thirty feet above the waterline because the ship was riding empty. For the same reason, the *Tarquin Dell* was difficult to maneuver in the storm and was prone to heavy rolling. The captain managed to turn it beam-on to the waves in an attempt to shelter the waters on the downwind side. The lifeboat circled around the stern and tucked in close against the ship's hull. Far above, on the *Tarquin Dell*'s deck, sailors in life jackets stood along the railing, holding on against 30-degree rolls and attempting to lower light "heaving lines" to which the lifeboat's bow and stern lines might be secured. This proved almost impossible to accomplish. The *Tarquin Dell*'s sailors were trying to tie one-handed knots on a rolling deck, and the few lines that they did secure broke. They kept at it. The situation in the lifeboat was nearly uncontrollable. Many of the crewmen were crying and shouting, and the boat was brutally slamming against the ship's unyielding hull. At the lifeboat's bow, Uddin broke a boat hook while fending off and then continued to work with the stub. The storm waves seemed to be undiminished by the *Tarquin Dell*'s mass. One of the waves rose so high that it came within a foot of simply depositing the lifeboat on the ship's deck. But then the boat dropped away, and the final line broke. The boat started drifting rapidly forward, and the *Tarquin Dell*'s crew ran along with it, until one of them heaved a heavy line into the center of the crowd below.

At that point things went very wrong. Rather than securing the line to prevent further drift, a cluster of desperate men grabbed it, each higher than the last, until very quickly they were standing, half hanging from the line, and unbalancing the lifeboat. Again Third Officer Romal shouted desperately, "Sit down! Calm down!" But then a large wave broke over the boat, and the boat swamped and tilted, and all but one man, who was sitting toward the stern, were washed into the Atlantic Ocean.

Despite their life jackets, most of the men seem to have gone deep. The gray-haired Spaniard José Manuel Castineiras felt the tangle of flailing legs and arms as he fought his way back to the surface. When he emerged, he saw that the lifeboat was flooded and floating low in the water, and that the man who had not washed out was still sitting upright in place, but whether because he had suffered a heart attack or a blow to the head, he was dead. He was a Pakistani "galley boy," fifty-some years old, and the first of the *Kristal*'s crewmen to die. Castineiras swam to the lifeboat and somehow crawled in. Several others followed. The *Tarquin Dell* had pivoted in the wind and drifted some distance away, and it was no longer providing protection from the storm.

Rolling heavily, it began a series of difficult maneuvers to set itself up for another try.

When Naeem Uddin was washed out of the lifeboat, he heard the screams of others before the ocean closed over his head. Time then slowed for him. He felt himself sinking as his life jacket started sliding up his chest. Astoundingly, like other life jackets provided by the *Kristal*, it was not equipped with a crotch strap. He grabbed the life jacket with both hands before it escaped over his shoulders, and he rode it to the surface. When his head emerged from the water, he found himself in a wilderness of waves, with neither the ship nor the lifeboat in sight. Three other crewmen floated within view, including the burly, black-bearded pumpman, Infante Casas.

The ocean was shockingly cold. Eventually, from the top of a large wave, Uddin spotted the swamped lifeboat and in the background the *Tarquin Dell*. Holding his life jacket to his chest with one hand, he began to swim. He had on his nightclothes, his heavy sweater, his coveralls, and his shoes. He used an improvised sidestroke, and because of the life jacket, he stayed mostly on his back. This meant that when occasionally he caught sight of the lifeboat, it appeared upside down and above his head. He navigated by those sightings. He swam for fifteen minutes or more, past crewmen floating helplessly. At times he cried. He knew he was going to die, and he wondered what it would be like, whether he would feel pain. The cold water had hurt him at first, but it no longer did. He had visions of his mother, his father, his sister, his brothers. He recited a Muslim prayer in preparation for the end. He said, "There is no god but God, and Muhammad is the last prophet of God." When he got to the lifeboat, he noticed that it was riding nose high in the water because there were five men in it, including Castineiras and the dead galley boy, and they were all sitting at the stern. Uddin tried to crawl aboard, and he was surprised to find that he lacked the strength. He hung on to a rope until he found a way to drape himself over the lifeboat's gunwale and roll in.

Later, another Pakistani sailor arrived, and Uddin helped him aboard. They sat toward the bow for balance. The waves were relentless. There were seven people in the lifeboat—which meant that eighteen remained in the water, though most of them were no longer in view. The *Tarquin Dell* was back in action, providing its limited lee shelter, now with an innovation: a heavy rope strung in a loop from bow to stern, to which the men in the water could cling, and the lifeboat could be attached. But the situation was grim. Uddin and Castineiras both saw dead bodies floating nearby. For the men still alive, the *Tarquin Dell*'s sailors threw life rings into the water and dangled ropes and a rope ladder over the side. After a while Infante Casas swam up, holding his life jacket under one arm. Castineiras thought that Infante Casas got into the lifeboat, and Uddin thought that he did not. What is certain is that Infante Casas grabbed a dangling rope with his powerful arm, that a wave washed over him, and then he was gone.

It seemed obvious by now that others were dying too. The lifeboat was being repeatedly washed over by the waves, and was threatening at any moment to capsize again. Uddin realized he could not afford to be passive—that he would have to fight to survive. He slid out of the lifeboat, swam along the *Tarquin Dell*, and despite being slammed repeatedly against the hull, somehow caught the rope ladder and began to climb. The climbing was slow. Uddin's leg was badly cut, and it was warm with blood. The ladder swung violently as the *Tarquin Dell* rolled, and waves continued to clutch at him, sapping what little of his strength remained. About halfway up the side of the ship, bruised and battered and still vulnerable to the ocean's surface, he simply could not move anymore. He did not pray or think of his family then; his mind was empty. He hung on. Vaguely, he felt someone grab his collar from above. It was a strong grip, and he fainted.

When he regained consciousness a few minutes later, he was lying in a small room along with three other survivors—the only *Kristal* crewmen who ever actually found the sought-for safety of the *Tarquin Dell*'s deck. All of them were blue with cold. Someone gave Uddin a bowl of soup. Someone bandaged his leg. The captain of the *Tarquin Dell* came and said that a helicopter was on the way. Soon afterward, Uddin heard the whacking of its blades.

The helicopter was a bulbous Sikorsky, with a rescue diver and a winch. It had come from La Coruña, an old port city on the Galician coast, a half-hour flight away. The pilot was a local star, a man universally known by his first name, Evaristo. He went after five men still loose and alive in the water, winching them up in a double harness two at a time. Then he swung over to the flooded lifeboat and picked up the survivors there too. Castineiras was the second to last to leave. By then another helicopter was coming onto the scene. Evaristo flew his load of hypothermic survivors to the hospital in La Coruña. By the time they got there, one of them had gone into cardiac arrest; he was rushed into the emergency room and revived. Evaristo headed immediately back to sea to find the dead and search for the missing. The second helicopter meanwhile had easily retrieved Captain Marin and the *Kristal*'s chief mate from their life raft and had rescued the eight men in the starboard lifeboat too. Uddin and the three others aboard the *Tarquin Dell* were the last to be plucked from the scene.

In business terms, the damage control began within hours. As the crew recovered in La Coruña, at the hospital and a hotel, the *Kristal*'s managers sent a representative to the city and employed guards to keep unauthorized visitors away—meaning mainly the press. They hired a crisis-management public relations firm in London, issued a terse statement of regret, and endured a few days of national coverage in Spain before the news of the disaster faded away. The survivors were rapidly repatriated to the far points of the globe and were paid their salaries to the end of their contracts, as the contracts required. The families of the dead were offered lump sums by the *Kristal*'s insurance company, in London. To receive this money, the next of kin first had to sign "quit-claims" promising not to pursue further action. Against the advice of the international seafarers' union, almost all of them signed. The amounts were kept private, and they involved commitments to silence, but it is known that most were small, that the payouts varied according to nationality, and that the Spanish got the most because before they signed the quitclaim, they made a little fuss.

The *Kristal* broke entirely in two and floated for several days until first the bow section sank, and then the stern. As for the human tally, eleven men had died, almost a third of the *Kristal*'s crew. Only four of the bodies were ever retrieved. Among those who were never found was Infante Casas. It seemed poignant and strange that the Spaniard had sailed the world for years, only to die here, off his own Galician shores. When Castineiras left the hospital in La Coruña, it took him less than an hour to make the trip home. But perhaps the saddest loss of all was that of the one sailor who by measure of his performance should have survived— the young, levelheaded Third Officer Romal. After he was swept from the lifeboat, he was never seen again.

The *Kristal* was by no means the only ship to sink that year. Dozens of other large ships were lost (hundreds, if one includes small merchant vessels), as they had been every year before, and have been every year since. During the 1990s alone, several thousand sailors died, worldwide.

The frustration is that a large body of regulations exists to keep such maritime disasters from happening. Most of the regulations are generated by a specialized United Nations agency called the International Maritime Organization (IMO), which is based in London and since 1958 has issued a plethora of technical standards for the maintenance and operation of large ships at sea. The IMO is a typically idealistic construct for bringing order to the world—a democratic assembly of 162 member nations, all of them determinedly equal, who work with the assistance of a technical staff and the consultations of accredited nongovernmental groups to establish regulatory packages known as "conventions," which the individual member states are free to adopt (or not) in their sovereign maritime laws. The enforcement of those laws is a separate question, and it is spotty, because the arrangement allows the IMO no enforcement powers of its own. Most of the individual states have neither the expertise nor the inclination to enforce their own official standards, and they rely instead on independent technical organizations known as "classification societies," which are not hired by the states, but rather selected and paid for by each ship's owner. Considerations of conflict of interest are not allowed to intrude. Nonetheless, the IMO has been influential and indeed has become the universal reference for life at sea. Thumbing through the international conventions, hefting the books of regulations, or browsing the logbooks and certificates required to be carried aboard a ship, one might easily conclude that thanks to good government in London, the situation is completely under control.

In other words, the ocean looks tight in print, much as many increasingly ungovernable nations still do by formal description. The problem, as some insiders will admit in private, is that the entire structure is something of a fantasy floating free of the realities at sea. Worse, from the point of view of increasingly disillusioned regulators, the documents that demonstrate compliance are used as a façade behind which groups or companies can do whatever they please. This does not mean that the paperwork is counterfeit—which is one of the more unimaginative concerns of U.S. officials with whom I've spoken. Far from it; the documents are as authentic as can be. The *Kristal* illustrates the point. It was designed, built, and maintained to full IMO standards, and it operated under the well-known maritime authority of a modern democratic state. It passed both scheduled and spot inspections on a regular basis. It was supervised and approved by the Italian classification society known as RINA, one of the world's top five. Its IMO safety procedures were approved by Det Norske Veritas, the Norwegian classification society considered to be the best in the business. Its crew knew of course that the *Kristal* was an unsafe ship, rusting away beneath its paint, harried by its owners, and was probably, as a result, handled recklessly. But when occasionally the ship was boarded by official inspectors whose role in principle should have been to intervene, the crew treated them with the well-practiced wariness of the Third World poor toward the police—a superficial acceptance underlain by fundamental disregard. When I finally tracked down Naeem Uddin in London, he told me he had never even considered the possibility that I suggested to him—that in theory the inspectors were functioning on the crew's behalf. Two years after the sinking, he remained visibly traumatized by the experience. But he was pragmatic too. Indeed, he'd had a job precisely because the *Kristal's* inspections had meant hardly anything at all.

Two

THE WAVE MAKERS

For those of us who live ashore and are accustomed to the promise of orderly lives, it can be difficult to accept just how unruly the ocean has become. In earlier times, people were clearer about its savagery. For most of human history, with few exceptions, the open ocean was simply a forbidden zone, a place of horrors real and imagined, that was only occasionally crossed on accidental trips downwind, dangerously, and with no way home. The ocean was the great barrier isolating the continental populations and, incidentally, also protecting them from one another.

At the height of their power, the Romans declared the Mediterranean to be their "lake," and for a while they managed to treat it as such—but only until the empire fell apart. Permanent change had to wait another thousand years, until the age of European expansion and the birth of nations as we know them today. Ocean travel remained notoriously dangerous, but by the early 1600s it had become common enough that the Dutch East India Company felt compelled to hire a local lawyer named Hugo Grotius to write *Mare Liberum*, a carefully reasoned defense of international freedom on the high seas, based on concepts of "natural law." The immediate purpose was to counter impractical claims of oceanic exclusivity by the Spanish and Portuguese, and specifically to justify a Dutch privateer's 1602 seizure of a Portuguese galleon in the Strait of Malacca. Paradoxically, this defense of an act of piracy turned out to be the starting point for modern international maritime law. The freedoms insisted on by Grotius implied the need for limits that were eventually defined by a customary standard for territorial seas, a band of water three nautical miles wide, said to be cannon-shot distance from shore and therefore about as far as a nation without a strong coastal navy could expect to exercise control over foreign ships.

When you stand on a beach at the water's edge, three miles is where the horizon lies—and it is near. You can row to it and return in a very short time. This limit endured for centuries, long after cannons could reach much farther and indeed ballistic missiles could reach around the world. In the 1980s, when the global standard finally shifted to twelve nautical miles, the United States made a principled stand for freedom of the sea and retained the old, tighter limit for itself. This was partly because the U.S. government did not want its naval ships having to detour as they steamed around the world, and partly because "freedom" still looked like de facto control. But it was also because the concept of territorial waters has always been more about sovereignty in the abstract—the need to draw a line somewhere—than about the exploitation of resources (for which there are separate rules) or practical homeland defense. It is not even really about excluding outsiders, since one of its core elements, long insisted on by the great nations including the United States, is the right of "innocent passage," by which foreign ships in transit may sail through territorial waters freely as long as they do not pose an immediate threat to the security of the coastal state. The "foreign" ships that the great nations have in mind are of course their own, largely now naval, as they cruise around the world. In other words, like much of effective international law, "innocent passage" is really about power posing as principle.

That is not necessarily bad. It has certainly been useful for maintaining global order that would-be obstreperous governments clearly understand that any new policy of interference with ships transiting through the oceanic choke points—the straits of Gibraltar or Hormuz, or for that matter the English Channel—will provoke a strong naval reaction, and war if need be. But there is a problem too, which in recent years has become increasingly apparent on the ocean. Such understandings may work well in the relations between governments, but they lose their meaning entirely against the agents of chaos who have learned to belong to no nation, and to thrive on the very standards that governments want to enforce—the need for customs forms, mariners' licenses, and passports—or, more basically, on the "natural law" of the freedom of the sea.

In the 1990s, as the maritime disorder grew, officials had to struggle against smuggling and the occasional big oil spill, but they continued to see the ocean in tidy governmental terms as a place subject to civilization, where navies projected national power and merchant ships sailed, however reluctantly, under increasing technical restraints. It was a view of the world still possible at the end of the twentieth century—an illusion of progress and community that was demolished twenty-one months later, with the attack of September 11, 2001. Since then, in the United States, many officials have come to regard the ocean with grave concern, believing that a full-blown maritime attack would make those of September 11 seem puny by comparison, that such an attack currently poses the most serious threat to national security, and that when the attack comes, it will involve the use of merchant ships. They may well be right. Ships can deliver a big punch, and their importance to world commerce practically ensures that in the reactions that follow, major self-inflicted damage will be done. In any case, for officials now eyeing the sea, suddenly freedom no longer looks like control, and even a twelve-mile limit seems far too near.

Out beyond the horizon, there is evidence that al Qaeda and related groups are indeed nautically minded, and have been since well before September 11. On January 3, 2000, al Qaeda and some of its affiliates conspired to ram a fiberglass workboat heavily loaded with explosives against a U.S. destroyer named *The Sullivans* in the Yemeni port of Aden. The attack was aborted after the boat nearly sank under the weight of the explosives. The terrorists learned their lesson. Later that same year, in the same port, they loaded a boat properly and blew a forty-foot hole through the hull of another destroyer, the USS *Cole*. Seventeen sailors were killed, and thirty-nine were wounded. It was early October 2000—September 11 minus eleven months. In response, the U.S. Navy tightened its warships' defenses. Other than that, the attack on the *Cole* had little effect. Again the terrorists appear to have learned a lesson—possibly about the inefficiency of hitting purely military targets, glorious though such targets may be.

Two years later another small boat darted out from the Yemeni shores, and it exploded against the *Limburg*, a French supertanker loaded with crude oil. The ship caught on fire and spilled oil, and one sailor was killed. This time the damage was magnified by increases in insurance costs for ships calling at Yemeni ports, along with a corresponding drop-off in traffic, as a result of which the Yemeni economy has suffered. True, if the goal was to hit at the West, this hardly constituted a major blow, but the sophistication of the choice to attack a civilian ship was noted with concern around the world, and it spread damage merely by raising the question of what would come next. A cruise ship full of Americans? A European ferry? A tanker in the Strait of Hormuz? A freighter off Gibraltar? Already the navies of the United States and its allies have their hands full with escort duties and patrols. And the ocean is a very big place. With deliberate preparation and the occasional well-placed attack, a few men with small boats can keep the navies churning for years.

But the real concern is not so much the vulnerability of merchant ships as it is their use by terrorist groups. Osama bin Laden is said to own or control up to twenty aging freighters—a fleet dubbed the "al Qaeda Navy" by the tabloids. To skeptics who wonder why bin Laden would want to own so many freighters, the explanation quite simply is that he and his associates are in the shipping business. Given his need for anonymity, this makes perfect sense—and it reflects as much on the shipping industry as on al Qaeda that the details remain murky. Such systematic lack of transparency is what worries U.S. officials when they contemplate the sea. The al Qaeda ships are believed to have carried cement and sesame seeds, among other legitimate cargoes. In 1998 one of them delivered the explosives to Africa that were used to bomb the U.S. embassies in Kenya and Tanzania. But immediately before and afterward it was an ordinary merchant ship, going about ordinary business. As a result, that ship has never been found. Nor have any of the others.

One measure of American frustration is the executive order signed by President Bush in July 2002 that expanded the U.S.

Navy's authority to intercept merchant ships on the high seas. The target has always been larger than simply the al Qaeda fleet of freighters: the government maintains a watch list of several hundred suspect ships whose names are constantly being changed and painted over to avoid detection, and it recognizes that terrorists, with or without a crew's knowledge, may use almost any kind of ship, from a dhow to a supersized freighter. Therefore the search has been large—and enormously expensive. It has extended through much of the world's oceans and has been carried out by the navies of the United States and its allies. By rough calculation, NATO forces so far have intercepted more than sixteen thousand ships, and they have boarded and searched about two hundred of them. For all that, there have been only a few rather modest successes.

For example, after an operation in July 2002 that involved warships and airplanes from four NATO nations (not including the United States), four suspected al Qaeda operatives were found on a couple of freighters in the Gulf of Oman and were transferred to a holding pen at the American base in Bagram, Afghanistan. The following month, fifteen Pakistani suspects on another ship were captured by the Italians in the Mediterranean after the ship's captain grew suspicious and turned them in. The ship had been renamed five times in the previous three years, most recently as the *Sara*. It was flagged in Tonga and owned by a Greek who operated it through a company named Nova Spirit, of Romania and Delaware. American officials said that the company was involved in human smuggling, an allegation that the owner vigorously denied. According to the captain, the Pakistanis had joined the ship in Casablanca, at the owner's insistence. Though they had claimed to be seamen and had carried seamen's documents, they demonstrated no knowledge of ships, and to a man grew seasick when the *Sara* sailed through a storm. The captain said that they threatened the crew. If so, as terrorists go, they were inept. Because they were found with false passports, large amounts of cash, maps of Italian cities, and unspecified evidence linking them to purported al Qaeda operatives in Europe, they were charged with conspiracy to engage in terrorist acts. Pakistan refuted the charges and claimed that Italian authorities had bungled the investigation. By the following summer, the Pakistanis' plight had drawn the attention of human rights activists, and in June 2003 they were freed.

Italy took an even softer line in two other encounters. In February 2002, eight suspected al Qaeda terrorists disembarked from a Nova Spirit ship in Trieste with false documents and ultimately disappeared. A more bizarre case had occurred several months earlier, in October 2001, when port police in the southern city of Gioia Tauro found a forty-three-year-old Egyptian-born Canadian citizen named Amid Farid Rizk inside a Maersk Sealand container. Rizk became known as "Container Bob." His box had been loaded in Port Said, Egypt, and was being transferred in Italy to a ship bound for Rotterdam, where it was scheduled to be transferred again, this time for the final destination of Halifax, Nova Scotia. It is said that Rizk was discovered when the Italian police heard him drilling additional ventilation holes. He was a man who apparently liked his comforts. When he emerged, he was clean-shaven, neatly dressed, and obviously well rested. The container was equipped with a bed, a toilet, a heater, a water supply, a cell phone, a satellite phone, and a laptop computer. Investigators also found cameras; a valid Canadian passport; maps and security passes for airports in Canada, Thailand, and Egypt; a Canadian aircraft-mechanic certificate; and an airline ticket from Montreal to Cairo via Rome.

The use of containers to gain entry to North America is a well-established trick, part of the vast volume of human smuggling that relies on the far vaster volume of ordinary trade to penetrate the borders. And though the customers willing to transport themselves this way often arrive in very poor shape (sometimes dead), Cadillac containers like Rizk's have been seen before. Still, Rizk never adequately explained his setup or why, as a Canadian citizen, he had not simply flown. Upon his arrest he hired an attorney named Michele Filippo Italiano, whose services I can recommend. Italiano said that Rizk's decision to travel in a container was completely innocent: "He had fallen out with his brother-in-law in Cairo and feared he would be prevented from leaving Egypt." An Italian court released Rizk on bail in November 2001, at which point he vanished, leaving no trace.

In their frustration, U.S. authorities reacted angrily and remonstrated with the Italian government. But in a world of trouble, a more serious threat is posed by the inanimate cargo that containers may hold. The fear on everyone's mind is that a nuclear device or some other weapon of mass destruction will pass through a port with little chance of being discovered, and will subsequently be carried by truck or train with dead-on precision to any target desired. Despite their expanded ability to run intercepts, there is very little that the allied navies can do about it. Aboard the transporting ships, the containers are stacked tightly and high, and most are impossible to get at. Moreover, speed is the essence of the container business: the ships move fast and on schedule, and any act of interference that did not immediately produce results would raise an outcry not just among shipping companies but among manufacturers and businesses of many sorts in every corner of the world. Without absolutely certain intelligence—there is a specific device, in a specific box, on a specific ship—the navies simply can't get in the way. This leaves NATO, in its hunt for terrorists, probing through the murk among all the other kinds of ships that could carry equally dangerous cargoes. Intercepts have produced results—most significantly a cargo of centrifuge parts discovered in October 2003 on a German ship bound for Libya, and its now-dismantled nuclear weapons program. But so far no terrorist weapons or devices have been found. And this is hardly a surprise.

For the hunters, the most promising moment came early in the chase, in December 2001, when intelligence sources reported that a freighter of uncertain description had rounded the horn of Africa and was bound for the Thames and the City of London, carrying a large chemical bomb. Whether the bomb consisted of the ship itself, loaded with volatile cargo, or of a dedicated device carried in its holds, such an attack was another of the nightmares on people's minds. One of the largest man-made explosions of the pre-nuclear age occurred in Halifax harbor on December 6, 1917, after a French munitions ship collided with a Norwegian freighter. The French ship caught on fire, drifted to the city's waterfront, and blew up. Witnesses said that the sky erupted in a cubic mile of flame, and for the blink of an eye the harbor bottom went dry. More than 1,630 buildings were completely destroyed, another 12,000 were damaged, and more than 1,900 people died. Now, with the possibility of a dedicated attack on London, a ship roughly matching the intelligence description was discovered steaming northbound through the English Channel. It was the *Niva*, an Indian bulk carrier with a declared cargo of refined sugar, which it intended to take up the Thames to a refinery near London's Canary Wharf financial district. British antiterrorist teams boarded it and for three days searched the ship for a bomb—no small matter among the sugar mountains in the holds. Eventually they concluded that sugar was all that the ship carried, and they allowed it to proceed upriver and to unload. Were they disappointed or glad? London was saved because the intelligence was false. The navies meanwhile continued their hunt, as they do today. The idea is to keep the pressure on, they say. Officials have begun to explain the lack of results as a measure of success.

The truth is that naval patrols hardly matter at all. It's not that they are a bad thing, or might not occasionally turn something up, but that they are national tools best applied against nations, and they have little effect against ephemeral gangs on the open ocean. This may be difficult to grasp, because a warship coming over the horizon does instill fear, and the struggle against al Qaeda is too young to make the lack of deterrence clear. But there is longer-standing evidence that can be brought to bear: the growth and persistence of a modern form of extra-national piracy that plagues large swaths of the ocean and has escaped every sea-based effort at control. On a global scale, this sort of piracy is more a nuisance than a threat, and typically it has been overblown in the press, but it is a significant phenomenon nonetheless, because it requires no base and it mimics normal operations where even legitimate ships fly false flags and swap names. Though it is apolitical by nature, it is structurally very similar to the stateless terrorism now faced by government forces.

These pirates are ambitious and well organized, and they should be distinguished from the larger number of petty oppor-

tunists whose presence has always afflicted rei
coastlines, and whose acts inflate the piracy statistics, but who lack
the criminal sophistication to steal more than they can load onto a
small boat—some of the ship's stores, or the cash and valuables of
the crews on board. Though they may be murderous—and do occasionally strike terror into the Western middle class with their
attacks on wandering yachts—these small-time pirates are as insignificant historically as street criminals in dangerous city neigh-
borhoods. A distinction should also be made from the famous
"privateers" of old, state-sanctioned agents who were used by governments to attack competing states at a time when merchant
sailors resolutely flew their national flags and modern nations were
on the rise. The new pirates, by contrast, have emerged on a post-
modern ocean, where identities have been mixed and blurred and
the rules of nationality have been subverted. Scornful of boundaries, these ambitious pirates are organized into ephemeral multi-
ethnic gangs that communicate by satellite and cell phone and are
capable of cynically appraising competing jurisdictions and laws.
They choose their targets patiently, and then they assemble, strike,
and dissipate. They have been known to carry heavy weapons, including shoulder-launched missiles, but they are not determined
aggressors, and they will back off from stiff resistance, regroup,
and find another way. Usually they succeed with only guns and
knives. Box cutters would probably serve them just as well. Their
goal in general is to hijack entire ships: they kill or maroon the
crews, sell the cargoes, and in the most elaborate schemes turn
the hijacked vessels into "phantoms," which, posing as legitimate
ships with all the requisite paperwork, pick up new cargoes and
disappear.

Owing to the scope of their ambitions, these gangs are responsible for the theft of much of the cargo stolen on the high seas, though they seem to perpetrate relatively few attacks. Given the murkiness of the world they inhabit, the numbers are difficult to calculate. Of 1,228 pirate attacks reported worldwide from 1998 through 2002, about a fourth were on ships under way, and of those about 68 were major, involving gangs of ten pirates or more. It's safe to assume that some in the gangs were repeat offenders. Among them during the five years in question they hijacked perhaps twenty-five large ships. The violence was not evenly distributed throughout the world. Though piracy posed problems off the coasts of South America, Africa, and the Indian subcontinent (and occurred in the very midst of NATO's sea hunt for al Qaeda), roughly two-thirds of the activity was concentrated in just one region—the area of the South China Sea, including the waters of Indonesia and the Philippines. The problem, in other words, would seem finite. Gazing at a map from the confines of land, one might think that with some sea and air patrols, and maybe the "expanded authority" to perform intercepts at sea, order could be imposed. But that authority already exists, and those patrols are being run, and the numbers have only wavered, and order has not come.

Paradoxically, the place in the region that ought to be the easiest to police is in fact the one most plagued by piracy. It is the Strait of Malacca, a narrow waterway roughly 550 miles long, flanked by tidy Singapore and Malaysia on one side and chaotic Indonesia on the other. Because it provides a shortcut between the Pacific and Indian oceans, as many as several hundred ships pass through it every day, most of them hard-pressed as usual to save time. Merchant crews understand the dangers there, and they know to post additional lookouts when sailing through. On some ships they even train to repel boarders and to fight them with high-pressure fire hoses if they reach the deck. But the crews are often shorthanded, and they may be too overworked to bother with training exercises of any kind, beyond the minimal safety drills, and too tired to stand careful guard.

Crew fatigue certainly appears to have played a role in the all too typical saga of the *Alondra Rainbow*. It was a nearly new 370-foot general-cargo vessel owned by a one-ship company in Japan through a subsidiary in Panama, where it was registered. Its design was conventional, with a raised bulwark at the bow, two main cargo holds, and a superstructure aft that rose five levels above the deck. The bridge spanned the ship, sixty-four feet from side to side, with outside wings from which close waters could be watched. From bow to stern it was a trim and functional ship. The bottom was red, the sides dark blue, the cranes and derrick beige, the superstructure white. The funnel was painted in broad stripes—blue, white, red, white, and blue again. The stripes were a whimsical touch. The *Alondra Rainbow* was a young ship, and as ordinary freighters go, it was jaunty.

In the fall of 1999 it was engaged in the tramp trade, picking up cargoes where it could, working primarily between the Malay Archipelago and Japan. It was crewed by fifteen Filipinos under the command of two Japanese officers—a sixty-eight-year-old captain named Ko Ikeno, and a chief engineer named Kenzo Ogawa, who was sixty-nine. Both officers were lifelong seamen. Captain Ikeno had graduated from the Tokyo University of Fisheries and had gone to sea when he was twenty-five, in 1956. Eleven years later he had assumed his first command, and with the exception of four years spent on land, he had inhabited the ocean ever since, serving as the master of cargo ships, and trading in various corners of the world. Although Ikeno was a more careful captain than was Allen Marin of the *Kristal*, fundamentally he was a typical merchant master—not some distant authority figure with braid on his shoulder, but a modestly paid workingman in ordinary clothes, a technician whose thinking had been subtly elevated by the responsibilities that he bore. It is not clear whether Ikeno ever loved the ocean; few merchant mariners do for long. Later it certainly came to terrify him. But, like others, he had a family ashore, and he was a reliable, stolid man who happened to make his living this way.

On the morning of October 17, 1999, after an uneventful crossing of the Java Sea, the *Alondra Rainbow* arrived with empty holds at the outer anchorage of Kuala Tanjung, an equatorial port dominated by an aluminum smelter on the Indonesian island of Sumatra, west and north of Singapore, at roughly the midpoint of the Strait of Malacca. Captain Ikeno posted a normal pirate watch through the night, and in the morning, he eased his ship into the port, to an assigned berth. Over the next five days the *Alondra Rainbow* took aboard a full load of 6,972 bundles of aluminum ingots, each bundle weighing about a metric ton, or 1,000 kilograms. The work was unhurried, as loadings go. It was supervised by the ship's chief mate, a Filipino with the musical name of Voltaire Lapore. The ingots weighed fifty pounds each. They were stamped with the letters I.N.A.L. for the producer, the Indonesian Asahan Aluminum plant, a sprawling coastal facility, 60 percent owned by Japanese, whose voracious requirement for hydroelectric power has denuded a huge swath of the inland countryside and earned it condemnation by environmentalists as a typically disastrous mega-project. Captain Ikeno had visited the plant the year before, without giving any evidence that he shared such concerns.

He was paid to be pragmatic. The cargo in his hold had a value of $10 million, which happened to be the value of the *Alondra Rainbow* as well. His job was to shepherd this $20 million package 3,300 miles north across the open ocean to Omuta, Japan, on the southern island of Kyushu. Once the ship was free of the Malacca and Singapore straits, the route would lead through the waters between the Malay Peninsula and the island of Borneo, across the South China Sea past the Philippines, past Taiwan, and finally across the East China Sea. This was typhoon season, and over the previous month a progression of tropical storms of varying intensities had been roiling the western Pacific, including a ship-killing super-typhoon named Bart, which in September had developed east of Taiwan with sustained winds of 150 miles an hour and higher gusts. However, such storms could usually be circumnavigated, and none were currently charted. The trip would require about a week. In preparation, Captain Ikeno had the ship fueled.

As always, the air at Kuala Tanjung was hot and humid. Local chandlers came aboard with their supplies and paperwork, as did the port's hawkers, who scampered up the gangway and sold directly to the crew. The hawkers' goods were global things, like garish radios and running shoes, many of them stolen from other ships, though this could never be proved. They haggled in broken English, the language of the sea. It was a typical port scene. By late afternoon on October 22 the *Alondra Rainbow* was ready to sail. The sun set behind Sumatra at 6:06 p.m. Two hours later, after maneuvering to clear the dock, the ship got under way. By the time it cleared the outer anchorage and was headed down the Strait of Malacca, deep night had fallen. As usual, the crewmen were tired after a stay in port, as much because of the disruption of the watch-keeping rhythms as because of any work or drinking they might have done.

The bridge was darkened to allow the sailors on duty to see outside. Captain Ikeno stood duty there, along with the ship's third officer and a helmsman steering by hand. The steering was passive on such a calm night. Occasionally Captain Ikeno asked for a heading correction or a small turn. The *Alondra Rainbow* moved to the southeast at a moderate speed, barely trembling with the exertion. An almost full moon illuminated the waters from high overhead. The ocean's surface drowsed in the balmy air; it foamed with the ship's passage and rose into little waves in the wake, but shortly settled down again and slept. In the moonlight, that wake would have been clearly visible to anyone looking back from outside on the bridge's wings, but the seamen's attention was focused necessarily on what lay ahead. There were islands around, dark masses, some sprinkled with lights. Among them moved ships, ferries, and coastal craft—obstacles that appeared as masthead lights, or as ghostly shapes, or not at all. The smaller vessels would have been invisible to radar's searching eye, and even some of the larger ones might occasionally have been missed. As an experienced mariner, Captain Ikeno was aware of these dangers, but eventually he felt he had the necessary space, and he accelerated the *Alondra Rainbow* to its full 13 knots. At 10:00 p.m. he ordered the helmsman to switch on the autopilot and set in an east-southeasterly heading of 113 degrees, outbound for the Singapore Strait and the ocean beyond. Having reminded the third officer to keep a careful lookout for pirates, he left the bridge for his quarters, one deck below. He intended to relax, draft a departure telex to the ship's owners, and take a bath. A few minutes later, with the moon now directly overhead, the *Alondra Rainbow* came under attack.

The assault was not a casually opportunistic act—yet another case of native fishermen suddenly striking at passing wealth—but rather the culmination of an elaborate plot. The operational phase appears to have started nearly three weeks earlier, with a meeting in a coffee shop at the port of Batam, Indonesia, just across the strait from Singapore. At least two of the future pirates were there—a local resident and ship's engineer named Burhan Nanda and a Sulawesian named Christianus Mintodo. Both men were middle-aged. Mintodo said he held a master's certificate, variably from Honduras or Belize. Both men were short and slight but physically tough, and undoubtedly they had spent hard years at sea. Mintodo in particular had a dangerous air, a quiet voice and restrained demeanor belied by the calculation and ruthlessness that were evident in his eyes. It is presumed that he knew Nanda already, and that both men had been involved in piracy before. They were joined at the table by a recruiter for the current venture—an "employment agent" who is said to have gone by the name Yan, or Yance, Makatengkeng—who outlined the plan. Makatengkeng has since become a fugitive from Indonesian justice, though at little risk of being found. He was serving as an agent for the real power, an anonymous figure known simply as "the Boss." This man is believed by investigators to be Chinese, though such national distinctions mean little on the ocean today.

For the pirates in Batam, the Boss was a disembodied voice on a throwaway phone. He telephoned Makatengkeng at the coffee shop and welcomed the new officers aboard. The conversation would probably have seemed legitimate to anyone listening in. The words were those of an honest employer working through an honest agent to hire an honest crew: Christianus Mintodo was to be the captain of a ship, Burhan Nanda his chief engineer. The setup reflected normal arrangements on the high seas. All that was required was a slight shift of a word or two, or even an implication, to unleash the mayhem that followed.

Intricate planning was involved, most of it logistical. Mintodo and Nanda flew to Jakarta, on the northern tip of Java, where they hired a port service boat to ferry them to the *Sanho*, an old freighter lying inconspicuously in the outer anchorage. The *Sanho* was a pirate ship, pure and simple. It was financed by the Boss or his syndicate and commanded, allegedly, by a man who called himself Marnes Zachawarus and is now another fugitive from the law. While lying off Jakarta, the *Sanho* took on fuel and provisions. Over several days a crew of thirty-five pirates was assembled, including of course Mintodo and Nanda. Most of these men were Indonesian, but they included Chinese, Malaysians, Thai, and perhaps other nationalities. They were divided into groups according to skill and function. The hijacking team was made up of fifteen armed men equipped with a fast boat that probably was stowed somewhere aboard.

On October 16, 1999, after receiving a satellite call from Makatengkeng, the *Sanho* left Jakarta and headed upcoast for the port of Kuala Tanjung. It arrived there on the night of October 21 and lingered in the outer harbor. The next day, word came from a port informant that the *Alondra Rainbow* would depart around sunset. The timing was convenient. There is a theory that one of the pirates may have gone aboard when the ship was berthed, perhaps by posing as a hawker, and that he hid himself away in order later to emerge and lower ropes to the others. But the hijacking team consisted of nimble men who would have had no trouble securing grapples and ropes on their own, and who were practiced at the art of shinnying barefoot up bamboo poles. It is unknown how they actually proceeded, though it seems likely that the *Sanho* put to sea first, that it was one of the ships the *Alondra Rainbow* passed by on the sleeping moonlit ocean, that the pirates approached from behind in their small fast boat, and that while the *Alondra Rainbow* plowed ahead under autopilot at 13 knots, they easily climbed onto its stern.

Despite his earlier warning to the ship's third officer—or maybe because of it—Captain Ikeno was taken unawares. At 10:30 p.m. he had not yet started his bath and was at work at his desk one level below the bridge, writing out the expected departure telex to the owners, when he noticed thumping on the deck overhead and simultaneously heard garbled shouts on the intercom. He rushed up the stairs and found that the bridge door was blocked from the inside. When he shoved at it hard enough to force a small opening, he saw pistols and knives, and he wisely desisted. The pirates yanked the door open, pushed him against a wall, and held a knife to his throat. In the same thick English used to haggle for goods, they threatened to kill him if he resisted. One of them fired several rounds into the ceiling to make the English clear.

There was a sign on the bridge that read SAFETY FIRST in block letters. But of course safety is a relative condition. Though the *Alondra Rainbow* was proceeding unmanned and at full speed through some of the busiest waters in the world, Captain Ikeno was occupied with more immediate concerns. He counted about ten pirates on the bridge, armed with knives, guns, and bolo swords. They went barefoot and wore ski masks and loose clothes. From their language and build and what he could see of their skin, he thought they included both Malaysians and Indonesians. They had roped the hands of the third officer and the helmsman behind their backs, and they did the same now to him. Ikeno was afraid of their tempers, and he did not speak. One of the pirates took his wristwatch, and another took the ship's master key out of his pants pocket. They then forced him to guide them through the accommodation decks, where they pulled terrified sailors out of their cabins, bound and blindfolded them, and sent them to be held in the crew's messroom.

Captain Ikeno's fellow Japanese officer, the aging chief engineer, tried desperately to hold his cabin door closed from within, but he was quickly overpowered. The third engineer was on duty deep in the engine room, working in cacophonous isolation, when suddenly the pirates appeared as if in pantomime, shoving the captain before them. They made the third engineer reduce the ship's speed, and then they bound and blindfolded him and shoved him up the stairways to the messroom. The entire crew of seventeen had now been captured. Captain Ikeno was led to his cabin and forced to open the ship's safe. The pirates grabbed the cash that was kept there—several thousand dollars in U.S. and Japanese bills—and took the crew's papers and passports and the captain's second wristwatch. They also ransacked the other cabins for anything of value, which wasn't much. They took the captain to the messroom, blindfolded him like the others, and threatened to slaughter everyone if anyone rebelled.

Ikeno and his crew had every reason to believe the threat. Merely one year before, in September 1998, a smaller Japanese-owned freighter named the *Tenyu* had gone missing soon after departing from the same port of Kuala Tanjung with a similar load of aluminum and a crew of fifteen. Three months later the *Tenyu* was discovered under a changed name and flag in a Chinese port, but the cargo was missing, as was the original crew, all of whom are presumed to have been killed. The strangers found aboard the *Tenyu* were arrested by the Chinese under suspicion of piracy, but because they claimed to have joined the ship legitimately in Myanmar, and because they possessed used airline tickets to Rangoon along with valid Myanmar visas issued in Singapore, the Chinese authorities released them for lack of evidence. In the background was the understanding that they had not committed any crime in China. For Captain Ikeno and the crew sitting captive in the *Alondra Rainbow*, it was probably just as well not to know that at least one of the pirates on their ship had been among those released by the Chinese.

It is not clear whether the designated captain, Christianus Mintodo, had yet come aboard, or who exactly was on the bridge, but it seems likely that the *Alondra Rainbow* was again under control and being steered by experienced hands. Was it midnight now? The captive crew sat in blindness on the messroom floor, each man in isolation, feeling the familiar vibrations of the ship in motion. Because there were guards in the room, they did not talk. Captain Ikeno tried to keep track of time. A couple of hours after being shoved into the room, he noticed a change in vibration, which he recognized as a reduction in speed, and he heard a pump start up. He then felt a sharp bump. Soon afterward the pirates began to take the men, still bound and blindfolded, one by one from the room.

They were led down the corridor, through a door, and out onto an aft deck, to the railing. It was a very bad moment. The captives

must have felt near the end of their lives. But the pirates, rather
than shoving them overboard, removed the blindfolds from their
eyes. Ikeno found himself looking three feet down onto the deck
of a small freighter that had come up alongside. There were
armed men aboard—too many to count. With his practiced eye,
Ikeno saw in the moonlight that the ship alongside was rusty and
badly maintained, and that it was riding high, as if its holds were
empty. It was probably the original pirate vessel, the *Sanho*, commanded by Marnes Zachawarus. In his mind Ikeno dubbed it "the
dirty ship," a name that has been used ever since. He and his crew
were made to jump down onto its deck, after which they were led
below to two separate cabins, where they were blindfolded again
and ordered to lie on filthy mattresses spread on the floor. The pirates warned them to be silent and said that anyone who tried to
stand or look outside would die. From the sound of things—the
occasional bump, the clatter of equipment, the voices of men
moving back and forth—the two ships lay together for another
hour or more. But the night was still deep when they drew apart
and went their separate ways.

For nearly a week Captain Ikeno and his crew lay bound and
blindfolded in sweltering rooms as the dirty ship carried
them northwest through the Strait of Malacca and on into the
vastness of the Andaman Sea. They were fed only twice, taken to
the toilet, and given dirty drinking water from a can marked ESSO
on the side. This last detail they learned from Voltaire Lapore, the
chief mate, who saw it from beneath his blindfold. As the blindfolds naturally loosened, others learned to see as well. Ikeno's vi-

sion got to be so good that he could discern among the pirates, and he was able to study the man he thought was the leader— about forty-five years old, five feet eight inches tall, muscular, potbellied, dark-skinned, with the features of an Indian or a Pakistani. The pirates by then were entering the cabins unmasked, perhaps because they trusted the blindfolds, or believed that their prisoners would not survive. There was no softening in their attitudes toward the sailors, no creeping acknowledgment of a shared humanity. The pirates continued to threaten Ikeno and his crew with death.

On the seventh night, the engine stopped. The pirates came to the cabins, took the *Alondra Rainbow*'s crew outside, and made them lie on the deck. The scene was similar to one that had occurred less than a year before, which the crew must have been aware of: a bulk carrier named the *Cheung Son*, loaded with steel-mill slag, had been hijacked on the South China Sea by pirates dressed in Chinese customs uniforms. The pirates had lined up the twenty-three crewmen and had systematically clubbed them to death before attaching heavy objects to their bodies and heaving them overboard. It would have been of little consolation to the *Alondra Rainbow*'s men, lying prone on the deck of a dirty ship in the middle of the Andaman Sea, that the killers had recently been arrested in China and a rare trial was about to begin. The men standing above them now were clearly not the sort to care.

It turned out, however, that the pirates had a different solution in mind. Rather than dirtying their hands with killings, they floated the *Alondra Rainbow*'s inflatable life raft, which they had purloined at the start, and with disregard for their prisoners' ultimate survival, they forced the crew to crawl aboard. Captain

Ikeno was last to go. The pirates cut the rope. The dirty ship
steamed away, disappearing so thoroughly into the night that neither it nor the pirates aboard have ever been found.

The crew felt little relief at having been freed. They were now
marooned in a crowded rubber raft, without effective means of
propulsion, adrift on the open sea. They had no radio or navigation gear, and they were completely lost, with no idea even of
what ocean they were in. The raft came equipped with the barest
provisions: a few cans of food, a supply of fresh water, a first-aid
kit, two sponges, two safety knives with buoyant handles, two bail-
ers, two paddles, ten signal flares, and a pamphlet of survival instructions written in English, which amounted to advice to avoid
drinking seawater and to stay out of the sun.

There may also have been something about the importance of
keeping up morale—but that was especially hard. For ten days the
crew drifted. Ten ships passed within sight and did not stop. All
ten flares were fired off. The water rations grew precariously small.
The crew caught a few fish, which they held up and squeezed over
their mouths for the juice that dripped out. As the days went by,
the men began to pray and cry. The mood grew so surly that Captain Ikeno began to fear that he and the chief engineer, as the only
Japanese in the raft, might be attacked and even murdered. He
formally ceded command—most critically of the water supply—
to his Filipino chief mate, Voltaire Lapore.

On the tenth day adrift, around noon, a small commercial fishing boat came into view. The stranded crew took off their shirts
and waved them in the air. The boat slowly approached. Several
times it changed direction, as if the fishermen were uncertain
whether to get involved. Eventually it drew to within shouting
range and stopped, maintaining a wary distance. Pirates were

known to have posed as stranded mariners to lure innocent vessels into traps. The men in the life raft could see that the boat flew the flag of Thailand. One of them shouted in English that they were fifteen Filipinos and two Japanese, that they were victims of pirates, and that if they were not rescued, they would die. The fishermen might have understood a few key words. They remained suspicious and shouted back, demanding passports. It was an odd request, since pirates have passports too, sometimes in abundance, but this was not the moment for a debate. The immediate problem was of course that the crew's passports had been stolen. One man had an expired passport tucked away in his clothes, and he held it up. The fishermen were not convinced, but finally their skipper grudgingly allowed Captain Ikeno, alone, to climb aboard.

Once on the fishing boat, Ikeno tried to explain what had happened, but he could not make himself understood. He wrote out his name and that of the *Alondra Rainbow* and waited while the skipper radioed the details to his company. The radio conversation was in Thai, unintelligible to Ikeno. It clearly reassured the skipper, however, and he gave permission for the remaining crewmen to come aboard. The next day, they arrived at the Thai resort island of Phuket, where amid all the beach hotels and sunburned vacationers they finally stepped ashore. It was November 9, 1999, eighteen days after the attack. The Filipinos flew to the Philippines, where, for want of better jobs, most if not all eventually hired on to other ships. Captain Ikeno and his chief engineer flew home to Tokyo, and both retired from the sea.

The *Alondra Rainbow*, however, was still going strong. After the hijacking, Christianus Mintodo and his pirate crew sailed it brazenly through the Singapore Strait and across the southern edge of the South China Sea to the Malaysian port of Miri, on the island of Borneo. While under way they painted the hull sides black (a one-day job) and rechristened the ship *Global Venture*, a particularly apt name, which they carefully inscribed on the bow, the stern, and the superstructure. They also painted over the funnel's stripes—the blue, white, and red now becoming a single somber black. In the sheltered waters off Miri another ship came alongside and took on three thousand metric tons of the aluminum ingots—nearly half of the *Alondra Rainbow*'s $10 million treasure. The transfer must have required several days. The receiving ship was a freighter named the *Bansan II*. It sailed for Subic Bay, in the Philippines, where apparently it arrived renamed as the *Victoria* and presented satisfactory import documents for the cargo. The *Alondra Rainbow*'s aluminum was quickly sold for a small fortune. Attempts to recoup the loss by the insurance company bogged down in the Philippine courts. The local police mounted a criminal investigation of the *Victoria*, which went nowhere. There has been no prosecution of any kind.

Meanwhile, Christianus Mintodo on the *Alondra Rainbow* was suffering from a problem related to the sheer size of the heist—where to find a buyer for the four thousand metric tons of industrial material that remained in the ship's holds. Little is known about the tactics that he used once the *Alondra Rainbow* left Miri—only that the name *Global Venture* was changed again, to the *Mega Rama*, that the home port was shown on the stern as Belize, and that the ship steamed generally westward, either through the Strait of Malacca or by a more roundabout southern route, before finally gaining access to the Indian Ocean. One week after the hijacking, when the *Alondra Rainbow* had become overdue in Japan, its owners reported it missing. The meaning was obvious. From an office building in Kuala Lumpur a piracy-reporting center maintained by the international shipping industry sent out alerts and descriptions, along with notice of a $200,000 reward that was offered by the insurance company for information leading to the ship's capture. For days a search was mounted by patrol ships and airplanes from several nations, including Japan, but the *Alondra Rainbow* had vanished without a trace.

To the question of how an entire ship can disappear in modern times, the first answer has simply to do with the physical realities of the sea. To state the obvious, the ocean is made of water. The immensity of this simple fact makes it difficult to grasp. Ninety-seven percent of the earth's water resides in the sea in a molecular accumulation that fills the planet's lowest basins to an average depth of 12,234 feet. The molecules are heavy, weighing collectively about one metric ton per cubic meter, yet they are loosely linked and easily shoved aside. This is the combination that allows massive steel ships to float, as long as they are lighter than the volumes of water they displace. The water is heated by the sun, pushed by the winds, pulled by the moon, and slung around by the spinning of the earth. The sea is eternally restless. At all depths in all places it is constantly on the move in an interplay so large and complex that it has yet to be fully described, let alone understood in its effects. The point remains that the ocean is a fluid. And when a ship passes by, temporarily displacing some of its molecules, the surface immediately closes in behind and erases the trail.

This leaves anyone hunting for a ship to face the ocean's other simple fact—its surface expanse. The Indian Ocean alone spreads across more than twenty-eight million square miles, an area that is nearly twenty-eight times the size of India itself, more than seven times the size of the United States, and indeed seven million square miles larger than all of Eurasia. The Indian Ocean's western neighbor, the Atlantic, encompasses more than thirty-three million square miles—roughly the size of all the world's landmasses combined—while its eastern neighbor, the Pacific, is twice again as large. Of course, you don't have to search the whole ocean to find a fugitive ship, but searching even the relevant parts can be a daunting task. Patrol airplanes are expensive to fly and of limited endurance, and though the view they offer may stretch a hundred miles or more, against the scale of the ocean it is still a paltry thing.

The view from a chase ship moving across the surface is naturally much worse. In good weather the horizon line as seen from the bridge lies about ten miles away, and it imprisons even the radar with an enclosing circle that is impossible to get beyond. When the weather worsens, the circle constricts, until in heavy conditions the air thickens with blinding rain and spray, and the winds stir up great mounds of waves that rear above the horizon. In severe storms the waves pitch and roll even the largest ships with terrible violence, and the sea may rise higher than the bridge and sweep across the forward decks with unstoppable force, tearing off steel protrusions and compressing the horizon's enclosing circle until the last vision is lost and primitive survival is all that counts. I mention this as a reminder of the physical world in which the search for the *Alondra Rainbow* was carried out, which was not just some place on a map. In fact, there were no storms on the Indian Ocean in early November 1999—merely the usual slow swells stretching out to the horizons. But the *Alondra Rainbow* vanished anyway, because it is in the nature of the ocean that it could.

That a ship can hide in plain sight would hardly come as a surprise to the U.S. Coast Guard, which for years has been locked in a fight against smugglers skilled at pulling disappearing acts, and has had to deal as well with the reverse side of the magic trick—the sudden emergence as if out of nowhere of ships that may pose a threat, either because they are decrepit and may spill something or because they are involved in crime. The Coast Guard is a peculiar organization, a militarized hybrid that is as much a shipping inspectorate as a maritime police force. It consists of 5,700 civilians and 43,000 people in uniform, some of them wishing for battle but most of them not. As the only armed service required to reside outside the Pentagon, it has long been a bastard child, with a bastard child's complaints—lack of love, lack of funding—and it remains a little uncomfortable in its skin. But through difficult experience it is also very familiar with the interwoven disorders of the sea; and by chance of history now, with the United States facing this new form of oceanic threat, it is unexpectedly in a position unique among American forces of being able at least to respond in relevant ways. As a result, it has been shunted from the Department of Transportation to that of Homeland Security, given a bigger allowance, and assigned the lead role in protecting American shores. This may prove to be a thankless task, but the Coast Guard is basking in the implicit praise, and it has set diligently to work.

The challenge is daunting. The United States has ninety-five thousand miles of coastline and more than a hundred seaports capable of handling large ships. It is the most active sea-trading nation on earth, accounting for a large percentage of long-distance maritime traffic worldwide and annually accommodating more than sixty thousand port calls by oceangoing ships, the great majority of which are foreign flagged, owned by offshore companies, and crewed by anonymous sailors—almost all of whom come from troubled parts of the world where America is resented, corruption is rife, and authentic documentation can easily be bought. These sailors necessarily bypass all the standard screening procedures by immigration authorities and arrive with their vessels in American ports. It is believed that in the past many jumped ship, though how many is unknown because the captains had no reason to report their losses to authorities on the shore. Procedures have tightened somewhat now, but the United States remains utterly dependent on these crews, trust them or not. Their ships bring in 6 million containers a year, 3.7 million vehicles, 53 percent of the nation's oil, and mountains of other goods and materials too numerous to name; and they take away significant amounts as well. They carry more than three-fourths of American foreign trade as measured by weight, and somewhat less than half as measured by value. Interrupt the flow with a terrorist attack, and the backup would instantly reach around the world, with devastating results. Institute heavy-handed inspections and other procedures to head off an attack, and the damage could be even worse.

The Coast Guard has no choice but to move gingerly. It has followed a logical path, starting with tightening the security of the largest ports by means of harbor patrols, cruise-ship escorts, civilian-based "harbor watches," better fences, and tighter gate and ship-access controls. The costs of the effort have been high, grossly estimated in the billions so far, and as the controls have expanded, ferrymen, tour-boat operators, and others have begun to object to the burden of expensive and inconvenient restrictions. Still, if safety has no price and is defined narrowly, the improvements have been real: ports, waterfront facilities, and ships in harbor are certainly better protected now against land-based or small-boat attacks. None of this, however, does much to address the more serious threat of a heavy maritime attack—a ship that delivers a weapon, for instance, or simply steams in and blows itself up. The desire for funding and power is typically difficult to differentiate from genuine patriotic concern, but the vulnerability is real, and Coast Guard officials make the valid point that by the time a ship pops over the horizon and pulls into port, little defense is possible. The problem is that popping over the horizon is what inbound ships just naturally do. The only solution is to push the horizon farther away—a Herculean task that Coast Guard members are now straining to perform. "Increasing the maritime domain awareness," they call it, borrowing unnecessarily from the Pentagon's pompous, self-indicting jargon. The Coast Guard has been aware of the maritime domain for years, and for better or worse they understand full well that as they push the horizon out into it, they are pushing into anarchy.

There is no obvious technological solution. With the exception of ten highly localized vessel-traffic services designed to prevent collisions in the major harbors, there is no U.S. coastal radar picket system, no maritime version of an early-warning system, for the good reason that it would be enormously expensive to build and maintain, and it would not be able to look over the horizon anyway. An additional problem would be informational clutter. One of the high-ranking officers I spoke to at the Coast Guard's Washington, D.C., headquarters laughed at the idea, often suggested by landlubbers, that radar could provide a panacea. He said, "We've got thirty million boats out there." Referring to the radar's adjustable sensitivity, he said, "Can you imagine how we'd have to turn down the gain?" That brought up the subject of attacks by vessels smaller than three hundred tons, the Coast

Guard's minimum definition of a ship and currently the bottom limit for much of the security thinking. It was a possibility that left the poor man shaking his head at the complications. He said that the Coast Guard was aware of the problem and would be turning to it as soon as it could. In any case, for the physical monitoring of coastal seas, alternatives other than radar are being pursued, including increased ship and air patrols, the use of surveillance satellites, and a hardwired shipboard GPS-based transponder system. This last, however, the shipping industry is resisting, arguing that it will reveal proprietary information to competitors and (less plausibly) provide targeting coordinates for attacks by terrorists and rogue states. All these initiatives will require years to implement, and even in combination they will leave loopholes big enough to steam a ship through. At best, the sort of information they can provide is crude—a ship by some name is approaching from some location out there on the ocean—and does little to answer the more important questions of who the owner is, who and what is aboard, and (the big one) how legitimate its intentions are. Transparency, in other words, will still be lacking.

The U.S. Coast Guard is also shoving at the horizon with a regulatory change: the requirement for a four-day advance notice of arrival, where before only one day's notice was necessary. This notification, along with a crew list, a cargo description, and several other details, has to be sent to a new Coast Guard operation in West Virginia known as the National Vessel Movement Center. For the Coast Guard, the term "movement" means merely the arrival or departure of a ship. But the center's name has ended up being an embarrassment: to outsiders it conjures up visions of a high-technology war room providing an omniscient view of the ocean, and this in turn requires the Coast Guard to explain that such views are not possible, and to explain why they are not. Where would you even start? The National Vessel Movement Center is an office full of clerks. They receive about six hundred notices a day, by phone, fax, and e-mail, and they enter the information into a consolidated database that Coast Guard intelligence and operations people can then contemplate, trying to discern which ships seem somehow out of whack—one that's importing wheat from Indonesia, for instance, or carrying an oversize crew, or maybe just belonging to Nova Spirit and flying Tonga's flag. The idea is to intercept, board, and inspect those ships while they are still safely at sea. Nationwide, this is being done on average about twice a day.

The U.S. Coast Guard, like the U.S. Navy, searches for bombs only on the basis of specific information, which does occasionally arrive, but so far has turned up nothing. For want of action, therefore, the emphasis is on the crews, particularly those from certain Muslim countries, who, in addition to being fingerprinted and photographed by immigration authorities upon arrival, are restricted to the ships while in port unless they have valid visas. It is said that this is a temporary adjustment until better crewmen's documents can be brought into play. There is unembarrassed talk in Washington of a future under control, in which sailors will undergo meaningful background checks and will be supplied with unforgeable, biometrically verifiable IDs by honest, appropriately equipped, and cooperative governments. Panama, for instance, will vouch for the integrity of, say, an Indonesian deckhand working on a ship operated by a Cayman Island company on behalf of an anonymous Greek. This is a vision so disconnected from reality that it might raise questions about the sanity of the United States. Back in the real world, the new guard services in ports are provided by private security companies and are paid for by the ships at the cost of thousands of dollars for a typical stay. The additional expense seems to be accelerating a global shift, already under way, from brown-skinned sailors toward the even cheaper Chinese. Domestically, the new procedures have brought a presumed reduction in ship-jumping incidents, which, if it has not measurably headed off terrorist attack, has at least forced would-be immigrants to jump ship elsewhere—say, in Mexico—before joining the crowds of unauthorized visitors coming overland into the United States.

Meanwhile, the Customs Service, now also a part of the Department of Homeland Security, has imposed new reporting requirements on inbound freight and has embarked with much fanfare on a container-security initiative, by which it is placing inspectors in twenty large ports overseas. Because the physical inspection of a container can take hours, only about 2 percent of the six million units headed to the United States each year are opened; but some can be scanned by X-ray machines or radiation detectors, and more can be looked over by experienced inspectors checking for paperwork anomalies. Still, the opportunities for something to slip in are innumerable. There is talk of equipping the containers with tamperproof seals and intrusion-detection devices, neither of which would stop the loading of a bomb at the outset or more than inconvenience a determined terrorist who wanted to insert such a weapon during a container's long voyage to port. I spoke to a Dutch maritime official very familiar with the U.S. effort in Rotterdam. He was sympathetic to the American plight, but he privately scoffed at the idea that the new inspections had any meaning at all. Speaking of just that one port, he said, "Look, if you want to send a bomb through, it's so simple! The chances of it being filtered out are almost nil!" He was not being critical so much as flatly descriptive. As a believer in good government, but long exposed to the chaos of the ocean, he seemed to have learned the hard lesson that government tools might simply not apply.

The Coast Guard struggles on with the tools that it has, as it must. Though its members tend to be alert and very aware of the complexities they face, as a collective, they are confined by governmental frames of reference. One sign of their confinement is the effort they expended in 2002 to create a new body of ship and port security regulations overseen by the very same institution that has proved incapable of controlling the situation at sea—the International Maritime Organization. As of July 2004, every ship above five hundred tons will have to designate a Ship Security Officer (SSO), who will work under a designated Company Security Officer (CSO) and be familiar with the new documents required to be carried aboard, including a Ship Security Plan (SSP), which is based on a Ship Security Assessment (SSA). The paperwork will be subject to the approval of each ship's flag state, which in most cases will rely as usual on the expert oversight (paid for by the shipowners) of the classification societies, which for these purposes are to be known as Recognized Security Organizations (RSOs). Another complicated set of rules and acronyms will apply to ports. The effect has been the instantaneous creation of a whole new industry, as tens of thousands of ships and mobile offshore drilling platforms struggle to get the paperwork done.

Close observers have been incredulous. Reflecting a widespread view, one of them said to me, "We're doing nothing but creating this pile of regulations. It's a small pile compared to other piles, but look what the flags of convenience have already done with those. Oh, on paper everything will be all right, but in reality it will not make any difference. And what is a flag of convenience, after all? It's an absolute nothing. In the worst cases it's just a commercial company running a registry. Money flows in, and certificates flow out. I don't want to use words like 'cowardice' or 'overreaction' to describe what the United States has done—just 'ineffective.' Because you can get all the paperwork you want, no problem. And it will not help."

He was probably right. The only sure effect of the new regulations is that legitimate operators, who do not pose a threat, will comply. But it is likely that terrorists will comply as well, and that, like many shipowners today, they will evade detection not by ducking procedures and regulations, but by using them to hide. This would be very easy to do. Paradoxically, when a ship approaching U.S. shores does not comply, it will be because it is a bumbler, and therefore almost by definition innocent. People in the Coast Guard know this: they are not protecting the shores from a random hundred-year storm, but confronting a calculating and adaptable form of chaos—an intelligent thing. In private conversation most continue to talk about "channeling the attack" or reducing the odds, but others admit that they may not have affected the odds at all.

Politically—and perhaps ethically—it is of course impossible to sit back and do nothing: the United States is a nation, and it has no choice but to act like one. And although minor successes tend to be portrayed as significant victories, there is no denying that determined policing does sometimes pay off, both here and abroad. It turned out to be helpful, for instance, that after the naval search for the hijacked *Alondra Rainbow* failed in early

November 1999, the hunt for the pirates did not end. With the description of the *Alondra Rainbow* widely disseminated, and $200,000 in reward money on the table, the piracy-reporting center in Kuala Lumpur received a plausible report of a sighting toward evening on November 13, a few weeks after the ship had disappeared. The report came via satellite phone from the captain of a Kuwaiti freighter named the *al-Shuhadaa*, which was sailing in international waters off India's southwest coast. The captain said that the suspect ship's name was illegible in the fading light, but it appeared to have been freshly painted; he gave the location, and he provided intelligence, apparently gleaned from his radar display, that the ship was moving to the north-northwest on a compass course of 330 degrees at 8 knots. The piracy center sent the news to the Indian coast guard and requested an intercept.

The Indians could have sat back and done nothing. The *Alondra Rainbow* was a Panamanian ship owned by Japanese, crewed by Filipinos, and attacked off the shores of Indonesia by pirates of uncertain nationalities. Its disappearance had no connection to India at all, and there was certainly no domestic constituency expressing outrage and demanding action. India, however, is a party to the Law of the Sea, a sweeping 1994 United Nations treaty (as yet unratified by the United States) that includes a paragraph encouraging nations to stop pirates on the high seas no matter where their crime took place. Old Indian laws to the same effect are left over from British colonial rule. More important, the news of the sighting seems at first to have been contained entirely within the Indian military, which, like other militaries, is eager to use the equipment that it has and to take action. The suspect ship had popped into view like a rabbit running across a field, and without the need for legal or policy thinking, the coast guard just naturally went after it.

A patrol boat named the *Tarabai*, with twenty-four men aboard, headed out from the southern port of Cochin and, early on the night of November 14, spotted the suspect ship on radar at a range of thirteen miles, ahead to the left. The *Tarabai* closed the distance until the ship's lights came dimly into view, and it hailed the ship repeatedly by VHF radio, demanding that it identify itself and reduce its speed. There was no response. On the possibility that the ship's radio had failed (which no one believed), the *Tarabai* flashed its lights and fired two yellow flares, again to no avail. The ship responded by turning 20 degrees left and increasing its speed. The *Tarabai* then fired six warning shots across the bow from the deck-mounted 40/60 millimeter Bofors gun, a modified antiaircraft cannon. The *Tarabai* settled into a safe position one to two miles away and shadowed the ship for the rest of the night.

When daylight spread over the ocean, the *Tarabai's* crew saw the ship clearly for the first time. It was a good-looking vessel, a giant compared with their own. Through binoculars they could see the name *Mega Rama* and the flag state Belize painted on the stern. In the early morning, a turboprop patrol plane, a German-built Dornier, flew onto the scene and joined the *Tarabai* on the VHF channel, calling for the ship to stop. This time a man answered, identifying the ship as the *Mega Rama*, with a cargo of aluminum and a crew of fifteen Indonesians aboard. He said that they were bound from Manila for Fujairah, an Arabian port. When ordered to submit to a boarding, he refused, informing the Indians that the *Mega Rama* had a schedule to keep, that it was in international waters, and that it could do whatever it pleased. This was hardly the sort of response one would expect from an ordinary merchant crew faced with a hostile naval force. Headquarters easily confirmed the lack of international records for a *Mega Rama* and from the ship's description concluded correctly that the *Alondra Rainbow* and its pirates had been found.

The patrol plane was lightly armed with a fixed self-loading rifle. On instructions from shore, it fired a few rounds across the *Alondra Rainbow*'s bow, and when that had no effect, it came around and hit the ship with five full strafing runs. For the pilots this was fine sport, and the high point of their careers, but for all the good it did, they might as well have been throwing stones. Low on fuel, they broke off and headed for home. The tenacious *Tarabai*, however, did not go away, and with permission from base, it began plastering the *Alondra Rainbow* with round after round from its Bofors gun. The shoot-up continued intermittently throughout the day, smashing the ship's windows and punching holes into its superstructure and hull. Still, the pirates refused to slow.

Later it was discovered that they had abandoned the bridge and had taken refuge in the engine room, safely below the waterline, leaving the ship to proceed on autopilot alone. They appeared to be trying to reach the territorial waters of India's arch-enemy, Pakistan, where their pursuers would dare not follow. When it seemed that they might actually succeed, India dispatched several warships, including a navy missile corvette named the *Prahar*, which arrived during the second night and added the threat of its heavier cannons to the argument. This did the trick. Around sunrise on November 16, having run from the *Tarabai* for thirty-five hours and nearly 575 miles, the *Alondra Rainbow* drifted to a stop.

Soon afterward a larger coast guard ship, the *Veera*, came onto the scene and found the *Alondra Rainbow* lying dead on a flat sea, with the *Tarabai* and the *Prahar* standing close by. Smoke was billowing from the fugitive ship's bridge and superstructure, and a group of pirates—all fifteen—stood at the bow waving white shirts and holding their arms high. Teams from the *Veera* and the *Tarabai* soon climbed aboard and handcuffed the pirates, including Christianus Mintodo and his companion from the Batam coffee shop, the chief engineer Burhan Nanda. They were transferred to captivity on the *Veera*.

The smoke aboard the *Alondra Rainbow* turned out to be from paperwork conflagrations that had been set by the pirates to destroy incriminating records. The fires were eventually extinguished. More seriously, the pirates had opened sea valves in the engine's cooling pipes in an attempt to scuttle the ship. They were nearly successful. By the time Mintodo and his men were safely under guard, the engine room had flooded and was starting to pull the ship down by the stern; had the engine room's bulkhead collapsed under pressure, the end would have come very quickly. The navy however sent in divers who managed to find and close the valves. Emergency pumps were set up on deck, the engine room was emptied, and the *Alondra Rainbow* was saved. The *Veera* was given the job of towing it 345 miles to the port of Mumbai, otherwise known as Bombay. The trip took four days, during which the pirates were interrogated. It is widely believed but officially denied that they were roughed up; one of them was somehow shot in the leg. A few of them are said to have made confessions, which were excluded from the subsequent trial.

When the pirates got to Mumbai, before being turned over to the police, they were displayed to the press, forced to kneel on the *Veera*'s deck, their hands bound behind their backs, while a proud and possessive coast guard commander in naval whites described their arrest as "the catch of the millennium." But the Mumbai police operate in a chaotic city of eighteen million people, with plenty of homegrown criminality, and they had a different view. One of their high officials later told me that the *Alondra Rainbow* was like an orphan dropped off on the doorstep. He said, "The common practice if such a ship comes, you shoo her away. Otherwise you don't know what to do with her. The question of jurisdiction comes up everywhere." The same was true for the pirates, criminals whom he called "the scum of the earth." What would happen, he asked, if India convicted and imprisoned them, but after their release Indonesia refused to recognize or accept them? There was little chance of that happening in this case, he admitted, but when the orphans were first delivered, the possibility had to be considered, if only in the abstract.

"What did you conclude?" I asked.

"That they would become stateless people." Then the problem for India, he said, would be where to send them. I suggested that they could be repatriated to their natural environment at sea. He smiled wanly.

In any case, the Mumbai police had no choice politically but to proceed with a prosecution. They held the pirates for two weeks at a harbor police station known as Yellow Gate, a dismal complex built in 1921, which contains five cells with wooden bars along a dim hallway and looks like a movie set meant to depict a Third World hell. Later the pirates were moved to the city's overcrowded central jail, where they were kept together in a high-security cell. As a group, they decided to grow their hair long. Meanwhile, in China, after a six-day trial, thirteen of the pirates who had attacked the *Cheung Son* and murdered its crew were sentenced to death. On the way to the execution ground, a group of them, who were drunk on rice wine, defiantly sang, "Go, go, go! *Alé, alé, alé!*," the chorus from a pop song called "Cup of Life." This got some press. The year 2000 passed. The *Alondra Rainbow* was eventually towed away by its Japanese owners, sold to a company in Singapore, and returned to service under a new name.

Justice moved slowly in Mumbai owing to the overload in the criminal courts. One of Mintodo's men grew sick, went to the hospital, and died. But early in 2001 the first depositions were taken, and the legal proceedings against the fourteen others finally got under way. It turned out that this was to be a landmark case, the first in history to use international law and specifically the Law of the Sea to claim "universal jurisdiction" for an act of piracy having nothing to do with the prosecuting country. There was a strange twist to the logic of the prosecution, however: though the act of piracy had given India jurisdiction, piracy in itself was assigned no penalties under Indian code, and the government therefore had to charge the men with other crimes. This it did with abandon, accusing them of multiple acts of armed robbery, attempted murder, assault, theft, forgery, and fraud—and even of entering India without valid passports, though they had done so involuntarily, in shackles and under guard.

The accused maintained their innocence throughout—a routine position in a country where no plea bargaining is allowed—but jailhouse informants have reported that privately they turned against Mintodo, their captain, who had assured them that on the high seas they could not be touched. It did not escape them that they were being tried to some extent for crimes committed by others—their fellow pirates on the "dirty ship" who had marooned Captain Ikeno and his crew—but this was not an argument that they could use. Their only lucky break was that none of the victims had died. India gave up the jury system in 1961, after it was believed to have failed. Most cases now are argued before single judges, who regulate the proceedings and ultimately hand down the decisions. The judge in the *Alondra Rainbow* case was a typically overworked officer of the mid-level sessions court of Mumbai. He was a kindly, mostly toothless man in oversize glasses, a Parsi named R. R. Vachha, who had a salt-and-pepper mustache and an upper gum that showed when he smiled. He had a reputation for patience, fairness, and competently written decisions. The courtroom over which he presided stood on the fourth floor of the old stone-built Secretariat building, from which the British once ruled Bombay. The room was large, dim, and, when crowded, as it usually was, stiflingly hot. It had three doors that opened onto a hallway, windows that had been painted over and remained closed, overhead fans that turned without moving air, a clock and calendar on a wall, several steel filing cabinets, a raised platform for the judge and his typist, a bar railing and table where the advocates presented their cases, an area of general seating where people waited for their scheduled appearances, and an enclosed bench in the back for the accused.

The pirates were brought to their hearings under heavy guard. Before entering the courtroom, they had to leave their shoes in the hallway, because defendants in the past had been known to hurl shoes at judges. The pirates, though, were well behaved, and some were almost gracious, as if they enjoyed these little excursions from jail. If so, they had plenty to enjoy. Had it run straight through, their trial might have lasted three weeks; instead it was squeezed among other cases a few hours at a time, and it dragged on for almost two years.

It was an unequal contest from the start. Serving pro bono as special prosecutor was an obviously brilliant attorney named S. Venkiteswaran, a master of law and argument, who at sixty-two is the preeminent maritime attorney in India and undoubtedly among the best in the world. He was assisted backstage by a protégé, a rising young attorney named K. R. Shriram, who, though not yet as wise and Churchillian as Venkiteswaran, is every bit as smart. Against this duo stood an ordinary public defender—a small-time criminal lawyer named Santosh Deshpande, who never stood a chance.

The questioning was excruciatingly slow. Venkiteswaran might ask, "Commander, where were you on November 15, 1999?" and the commander would answer, "I was aboard the coast guard ship *Tarabai.*" The judge would then repeat to his typist, "On November 15, 1999, I was aboard the coast guard ship *Tarabai,*" after which the next question would have to wait until the typing was completed. Nonetheless, over two years the prosecution brought in twenty-four witnesses and introduced a wide range of evidence, which, though circumstantial, led inescapably to the conclusion that Mintodo and his men were guilty. There were no defense witnesses at all. Deshpande wasted much of his work in formulaic attempts to question the identity of the captured ship and to discredit the integrity of the prosecution's witnesses, whom he systematically accused of lying. There may indeed have been some distortions in the testimonies, particularly about the pirates firing on the Indian warships, but Deshpande did not follow through on them. He was hobbled by lack of funds, but he also seemed to have forgotten that there was no jury to impress and that his job was to persuade a thoughtful and experienced judge.

The star witness was Captain Ikeno. Having been promised full-time police protection while in India, he came twice from Japan

to verify the real identity of the *Mega Rama* and to describe his ordeal in emotional detail. Venkiteswaran later said to me, "Deshpande was flamboyant and played to the gallery. But once the master
[Captain Ikeno] gave evidence, I was very sure no one could touch
the case. Look—you can ignore all the evidence that you have read,
and consider just the basics. Here is a ship with fifteen of the accused in it. They're caught. They've got a property which is hot. It's
proved beyond doubt that the vessel is the *Alondra Rainbow*. The
master's evidence establishes that he was deprived of possession
and control. Once that has happened, it is for the accused to show
how they came into possession of that ship. And if they don't show
it, then the presumption of the law is that they are the ones who
hijacked it. And no attempt was made to look into this aspect at all."

Deshpande occupied a difficult position. The pirates would
have made such poor witnesses that he did not dare to put them
on the stand. He was required nonetheless to support their claim
that they were an innocent crew who had been offered jobs by
manning agents in Jakarta and had flown to Manila and sailed
without any idea of the ship's ownership—or any curiosity about
the evidence, abundant aboard, that the vessel's name had been
changed twice in a few weeks. He also had to suggest that the
crew ran from the Indian forces fearing that the Indians were
pirates, and that the crew had no passports or seamen's cards
because the coast guard had thrown these documents overboard. Still, Deshpande's performance was weak. During his cross-
examination of a shipping expert from London, for instance, he
should have asked, but did not, "Sir, can you tell us how crews are
recruited for ships? Is it normal for sailors to ask questions of the
manning agents who offer them jobs? To know the ownership of
the vessels they serve on? To know the vessels' histories? Is it un-
heard of for a ship to change its name? To change its flag? To do

this at sea? Have there never been cases of pirates in uniform? Or of patrol boats being used?" The answers to those questions would not have turned the case, but they might at least have helped to educate the judge about some of the realities at sea.

When I met Deshpande, he turned out to be a youngish, beleaguered-looking man with a pronounced Indian habit of tilting his head to punctuate his words. He told me that his cases usually involved accusations of robbery, armed robbery, rape, murder, arson, and rioting. He said he had first met the pirates in court, on April 4, 2001, when their appeal for bail was denied. We talked about the trial. I asked why, if he believed the pirates' story, he had not put Mintodo on the stand. He said, "Basically the language was a big hurdle." I asked him if he had not at least tried to discover the identity of the manning agents in Jakarta. He said, "That is the police's job, to investigate." He told me that the pirates had trusted him, and that they still did. He said he had new information and was considering appealing the case, ultimately to the Supreme Court if necessary. Later, Venkiteswaran graciously offered to keep him company step by step along the way.

The pirates were convicted, of course. On February 25, 2003, Judge Vachha handed down a 245-page verdict, finding them guilty on every count except the passport violation and sentencing them to seven years of "rigorous imprisonment," of which three had already been served. Venkiteswaran was traveling at the time, but he was represented in the courtroom by his protégé, Shriram. Some of the pirates broke down, lamenting the fate of their families and the effect the separation would have on their children. Others remained calm. One of them came up and congratulated Shriram. Instinctively Shriram shook his proffered hand and then immediately regretted the contact, worrying that the man could have been carrying a needle and trying to infect him with HIV. He checked and found no wounds. From the back bench Christianus Mintodo looked on impassively.

Soon afterward I went to meet Mintodo at the maximum-security prison to which he and the others had been transferred— a nineteenth-century compound with fortresslike walls, in the hot and dusty city of Poona, about a hundred miles inland from Mumbai. The prison turned out to be a surprisingly peaceful place. Though filled to twice its designed capacity, it was noticeably less crowded than the city outside. I waited for Mintodo in a file room that opened onto the central courtyard, and I watched inmates languidly sweeping the walks with straw-bundle brooms or strolling by in small straight-backed groups, dressed in coarse cotton clothes and caps, talking quietly. The air in the shade was pleasantly warm. In the distance a prison phone kept ringing with a double ring, and it went unanswered.

Mintodo was wary when he arrived, and at first he pretended to speak little English. He was slim, barefoot, and copper-skinned—a man who at the age of fifty-six still moved with feline precision and grace. He had brought with him one of the younger pirates, Ari Kurniwan, age twenty-six, whose job was to translate and do most of the talking. We spoke for a while about the food and routines of the prison, the Indian guards, and the prospects for an appeal. I discouraged them from expecting results. We talked about the *Tarabai*'s attack, and the way that the *Mega Rama*, as they insisted on calling their ship, had trembled as it was being hit.

Kurniwan said, "We didn't know who was firing on us."

I said nothing.

Mintodo said, "At sea anything can happen."

About that I could agree.

I asked Mintodo why he thought Deshpande had not put him on the witness stand. He did not answer, but gazed at me appraisingly.

Kurniwan intervened. He said, "This idea is coming now in my mind for the first time!"

Later I asked about the manning agents in Jakarta, the key to their story. Kurniwan responded with a flood of words. "I come in Jakarta port. I meet a broker who says, 'Pay me two hundred dollars, and you'll have a job at three hundred dollars a month.' He gives me an airline ticket to Manila. It's my first flight, and I'm afraid of heights. I close my eyes the whole time. I go to the ship. This is my first job, my first flight, my first time going abroad. Everything is the first."

I said, "What was the name of the agent in Jakarta? I'll go there and find him."

Mintodo was looking into space somewhere above my head.

Kurniwan said, "When you come into a port, you find so many brokers. You don't have to ask their names. You trust them. They give you a job. They give an alias also, those people."

When I asked Mintodo for his contact there, he brought his gaze back down to me. He said, "It was the same agent in Jakarta. A broker. I forget his name."

It was all just a game anyway. Their agent was the one who went by Yan—or Yance—Makatengkeng, who had been at the coffee shop in Batam and had safely disappeared. He worked for "the Boss," who remains unseen and unknown and is presumably still active. Mintodo and his men were insignificant players on a very large sea—sailors who got stuck holding the loot long after the bigger players had covered their tracks. Piracy meanwhile shifts around and responds to pressures, but it either grows or remains essentially unchanged. It was clear in the Poona prison that the pirates understood this too. Their arrest and conviction had been proclaimed around the world as an important message that disorder would not be tolerated on the high seas. But they knew the ocean better than most, and they were just biding their time, unrepentant and undeterred.

Three

TO THE RAMPARTS

In principle, the leading industrial nations continue to promote the idea of the ocean as a governable place, and they actively participate in the IMO and the other diplomatic forums that are supposed to make it that way. In practice, however, they are rapidly backing away—recoiling from the growing chaos and attempting to build national defenses against the threat that it represents. The United States has pioneered this pattern for the past few decades, actively promoting new international regulations in London while simultaneously recognizing the weakness of the IMO and the United Nations and unilaterally imposing ever-stricter standards for ships coming to American shores.

Until the recent worries about terrorist attacks began to predominate, the U.S. enforcement effort was based primarily on concern about pollution, especially from oil. It began in 1977, after a disastrous winter during which as many as thirty tankers, most of them foreign flagged, came to grief off American shores. The most famous of those casualties was a twenty-three-year-old Greek-owned Liberian-registered vessel named the *Argo Merchant*, which had already been involved in fourteen incidents, including groundings in Indonesia and Sicily and small oil spills in

Philadelphia and Boston. It had been identified as an unsafe ship by the U.S. Coast Guard, which, however, lacked the practical authority at the time to exclude it from U.S. waters. In December 1976 the *Argo Merchant* left Venezuela bound for Boston carrying nearly eight million gallons of fuel oil. It had inoperative navigational instruments, obsolete and inadequate charts, and an incompetent, underpaid, and partially unlicensed crew. After a bit more than a week at sea, it ran hard aground against Fishing Rip Shoal, twenty-nine miles southeast of Nantucket, about twenty-four miles off its intended course. The crew was rescued successfully, but the ship could not be moved. For five days it sat there, battered by the waves, within view of television cameras, threatening the New England coast with an ecological catastrophe. On the sixth day it broke apart, spilling its entire load and creating a six-thousand-square-mile slick that—merely by chance—drifted out to sea.

It was not lost on the American public that the *Argo Merchant* was a foreign vessel sailing inside American waters, deriving profits from the U.S. trade but operating beyond Coast Guard control. In reaction, in the spring of 1977 the Carter Administration made the first moves toward defending the nation against the maritime free-for-all that the United States itself had helped to create. Significantly, it did not abandon the hope for international regulation, but pushed through a new set of global antipollution rules at the IMO in London and simultaneously gave the Coast Guard increased authority to conduct rigorous "port state control" inspections, in tacit recognition of the inability or unwillingness of the new Third World maritime nations (of Liberia, Panama, and so forth) to enforce safe standards on the ships that flew their flags. The port state controls constituted a retreat from the dreams of progressive civilization and world government; metaphorically, they were like drawbridges that could be raised to keep pollution away. Nonetheless, at first they were seen as temporary measures that would be necessary only until the "developing" nations had recovered from their colonial pasts and finished growing up. The American commitment to the IMO remained strong, and indeed the technical standards that the Coast Guard set about to enforce were the universally agreed-upon ones that in principle should have applied globally. It was still possible to imagine a well-behaved world divided among equal nations resolving their differences at the UN and sharing the values of the American middle class—the Jimmy Carter idea. There was a problem with Communism, of course, and there was the threat of nuclear war. But there was really no suspicion that ships like the *Argo Merchant* might be the vanguard of larger disorders to come.

In the 1980s, however, as ships flying flags of convenience began to predominate at sea, the "open registries" upon which the system was based mounted a coup d'état at the IMO and effectively seized control. Those registries were nothing more than proxy nations in the hands of the global shipping industry, and in governmental terms they were fundamentally corrupt. But because the IMO is funded by membership fees based on the size of the respective fleets, they were by then also providing most of the organization's financial support, and so they were able to demand access, denied to them before, to the technical committees where new standards were decided upon and the real power lay. In the framework of equal nations, Europe and the United States had no choice diplomatically but to give in. The U.S. Coast Guard continued to propose new regulations and to lobby busily for global maritime reform, but the IMO had been captured by the very forces it sought to regulate. It is not clear how obvious this was to U.S. officials at the time, so involved were they in the minutiae of the eternal negotiations. The forces of disorder rarely stood up and fought, but instead weakened the initiatives from within. As a result, much paperwork blossomed forth even as the chaos grew.

One measure of America's frustration was its long-standing in-ability to persuade the IMO to require tankers to have double hulls, a design meant to isolate the cargo tanks from the outer skin and thereby to add an extra level of protection against spills in case of collisions and groundings. Such a requirement would have been enormously expensive to comply with. Through its lobbyists and proxies at the IMO, the shipping industry fought back by delaying the issue indefinitely in committees and by raising tech-nical concerns (as it does today) about double-hull corrosion, hid-den leaks, explosive gases, structural strength, and the irrelevance of such designs to accidents that have actually occurred. These arguments had a certain narrow appeal, even gaining a natural constituency within the Coast Guard itself, where some of the specialists were inclined to agree that the double-hull initiative was being sold as a panacea. For those reasons, and because the U.S. regulations still closely followed the international rules, very few tankers in American waters were double hulled. But on the night of March 21, 1989, came the wreck of the *Exxon Valdez*—a 987-foot single-hulled supertanker that strayed out of a channel while avoiding ice and tore its belly open against submerged rocks in Alaska's Prince William Sound. The *Valdez* was American flagged and crewed because of a union-inspired law, known as the Jones Act, that prohibits the use of foreign ships in internal U.S. trade, in this case from the terminus of the Alaskan pipeline to refineries in California. Over the hours and days that followed the accident, forty thousand tons—nearly eleven million gallons—of heavy crude oil bled out of eight of the ship's eleven cargo tanks, poisoning a cherished wilderness for hundreds of miles around. It was a major environmental disaster. The consequences were large.

At U.S. Coast Guard headquarters in Washington, D.C., the man on duty in the safety office was a senior civil servant named Daniel Sheehan, who in retirement today works as a consultant to the registry of the Marshall Islands, a high-end flag of convenience based across the Potomac from Washington, in Reston, Virginia. Sheehan is an ethical and widely respected man. He recently told me that—having been through the *Argo Merchant* episode and the subsequent years of struggle at the IMO—as soon as he heard about the *Exxon Valdez*, he instructed the engineers in the office to examine the ship's plans to see what would have happened had the *Valdez* been double hulled. He warned them to brace themselves for a political onslaught, and he predicted accurately that they had at most a two-day head start on the angry demands for answers. But he himself was unprepared for the reactions that followed. When the engineers concluded that the grounding would have torn through a double hull as well, Sheehan prepared an overly technical briefing for the Secretary of Transportation, a political operative named Samuel Skinner, during which he described the relatively small gains, statistically, that could be expected from double hulls, and he patiently explained why such a design would not have helped the *Valdez* at all.

Skinner let Sheehan finish. Then Skinner said, "Okay. I understand that. Now, do you think we're going to win that argument with Congress?"

The only possible answer was a sheepish, "Obviously not."

This was yet another example of why technocrats are not in

charge. Skinner was not merely smart, but wise. Indeed, the American public and its surrogates in Congress got the story just about right: whatever the nautical details in Prince William Sound or the diplomatic niceties in London, and despite the well-known fact that "accidents will happen," something had gone very wrong at sea, and something very strong had to be done. Among the many changes that resulted, most of which did not address the *Valdez* accident directly, the most significant in global maritime terms was a further strengthening of the young port state inspection program for foreign-flagged ships, along with a parallel decision to assert American independence from the IMO by imposing an aggressive and unilateral phaseout of single-hulled tankers operating in U.S. waters. An additional requirement was put in place for ships to carry a certificate of "financial responsibility," guaranteeing that their owners could bear the cost of a cleanup should a spill occur. To some degree this had the opposite effect of the one intended: it drove the most dangerous operations even deeper beneath their layers of one-ship companies and offshore corporate veils. But the double-hull requirement was impossible to circumvent. The length of the American coastline in this case turned out to be an aid in its protection: it made no economic sense for the owners of single-hull tankers to deliver their cargoes to Mexico, for instance, because of the expense of overland transport, so if they wanted to serve the lucrative American market, they had no choice but to invest in double-hulled designs.

None of this did much for the world at large, since unsafe and aging ships like the *Kristal* merely went elsewhere to trade—a fact noticed with resentment in the less powerful countries exposed to their depredations. Nonetheless, it was out of practical necessity that the United States had retreated from the failure of internationalism on the high seas. For more than a decade afterward, its defenses remained tight, at least against disorder as defined by unsafe ships and the pollution they cause.

The same disorder laps against European shores, perhaps even more disturbingly, because of the tidiness there of life on land. For now as before in the United States the problem is seen in strictly maritime terms, and mostly as a matter of coastal pollution. Certainly Europe's history with oil spills has been a sad one. Among the many, too numerous to mention, was that caused by the wreck of the *Torrey Canyon*, one of the new breed of supertankers, Liberian flagged, owned by an offshore company fronting for Union Oil of California. In 1967 it rammed the Seven Stones Reef at the entrance to the English Channel off Land's End and lost its entire load of 120,000 tons of Kuwaiti crude—roughly three times as much oil as later spilled from the *Exxon Valdez*. The slick reached French as well as British shores. The IMO held a conference, but little was achieved. Ships continued to sink, and tankers to spill, among the growing crowds of vessels moving through European waters. Then came the big one: in March 1978, fifteen months after the *Argo Merchant's* grounding off Nantucket, at a time when the U.S. port state control program was getting under way, another Liberian-flagged supertanker, the *Amoco Cadiz*, lost its steering in a violent gale off the tip of Brittany near the French island of Ouessant. Eleven hours later, after multiple attempts to tow the giant ship to safety had failed, it hit the rocks and began to break apart, eventually spilling all 223,000 tons of the crude oil contained in its holds. The northern coast of

Brittany took a direct hit and suffered ecological devastation. Even as thousands of soldiers and civilian volunteers mobilized to clean up the mess, rioting broke out when people realized that their fishing and tourist industries had been wrecked. In abstraction they may have shared some responsibility for the accident—as consumers who drove cars and heated their homes with oil—but a ship's broken steering gear was precisely the sort of technical problem that, according to the IMO's logic, the regular inspections by Liberia or its agents could have caught.

In 1982 fourteen European countries finally got around to creating a regional system of port state controls, by which they agreed to inspect 25 percent of the foreign-flagged ships visiting their harbors, at first, as in the United States, to verify that they complied with IMO standards. Compared with its American counterpart, however, the European program offered a poor defense, and supertankers kept poisoning its coasts—in 1991, the *Haven* in waters off Genoa, Italy (144,000 tons spilled); in 1992, the *Aegean Sea* on the rocks directly under the lighthouse in La Coruña, Spain (74,000 tons); in 1993, the *Braer* off the Shetland Islands (85,000 tons); in 1996, the *Sea Empress* off Milford Haven, U.K. (72,000 tons). Smaller tankers and a large number of cargo ships of all descriptions sank as well. Europe's continuing vulnerability related to the lack of genuine unity between European countries, and to the fact that so many ports could offer good access to the same important markets: if Rotterdam grew too strict, the ships could shift their business to Antwerp; and if the Belgians got fussy, well, there was always Le Havre and the French. I've been told that in this competition the methods used to meet the quota were a reflection of the respective national characters—the Dutch, for instance, would perform proper inspections, but of the best ships rather than the worst; and some of the French would slyly fill in their forms without even going aboard, no doubt deriving a sort of vicious pleasure from the act. As for the Spanish and Italian inspectors, many could simply be bought off. Europe continued to pursue the internationalist ideal at the IMO because it really had no choice. But of course Europe was consolidating too, and if it was not quite catching up to the United States, it was keeping pace.

Then in December 1999 Europe experienced an accident that was similar in political impact to that of the *Exxon Valdez*. It was the loss of a smallish tanker much like the *Kristal*—a bottom-feeder named the *Erika*, nominally Maltese, that was owned by a single-ship shell company, inspected by the Italian classification society RINA, and manned by an underpaid and beleaguered Indian crew. Though it was nearly twenty-five years old, and the sort of ship one would expect major oil companies to avoid, it had been chartered by the French company TotalFina to carry twenty-two thousand tons of sludgelike fuel oil from Dunkirk through the Strait of Gibraltar to a power plant in Livorno, Italy. It didn't get far. In a storm off southern Brittany, having developed a leak and a list, it broke in two in international waters while running for refuge toward the mouth of the Loire. The crew was rescued uninjured, but both sections of the hull sank, releasing gooey black masses that rode beneath the ocean's surface as well as on it and, after drifting for about a week, began to hit the French beaches in noxious waves that drove France and its neighbors into an uproar. During the months of obfuscation and revelation that followed, people came to see the wilderness that was upon them. Merely establishing the true ownership of the *Erika* proved extremely difficult. The captain was jailed in France for more than a week. Upon his release he said that he himself had no idea who the owners were. He said that the *Erika*'s condition had been poor, and that he had dealt only with the ship's management company, Panship Management & Services of Ravenna, Italy, which incidentally, he said, had instructed him to run south for Spain after the ship's hull had started to crack. Panship worked for the ship's registered owner, Tevere Shipping of Valletta, Malta, which in turn was held by two other companies, Agosta Investments and Financiers Shipping, both of 80 Broad Street, Monrovia, Liberia. Somehow in the constellation of names behind this single ship there appeared to be still other companies—in Switzerland, the Bahamas, Panama, and England. There were various banks too, including one in Scotland and a Swiss branch of France's Credit Agricole. After a month of trying to follow these connections, the official French inquiry admitted defeat. It mentioned in its report that the *Erika*'s real owner might be an Italian family named Savarese—which perhaps exercised control through a Greek company—but said that none of this was certain. The report read stiffly, "The whole of this arrangement appeared complex to the commission. It ascertained that at the time of writing the present report, none of the legal entities or persons mentioned above had deemed it useful to manifest themselves to it, nor to make themselves known in any manner whatever."

But several days later (now a month after the accident) the great London-based shipping daily *Lloyd's List* discovered a stray signature that linked a Savarese scion, Giuseppe Savarese, to Tevere Shipping and the arrangement with Panship Management. Once asked, the manager of Panship Management was perfectly open about this. He said that he had called Mr. Savarese on his mobile phone within ten minutes of hearing that the *Erika* had developed a list, and that Mr. Savarese had been skiing at the time, at Roccaraso, in Italy. It turned out that Savarese lived in London, where he had a company called Ocean Breeze Navigation, a nice touch. It was his turn now to be open. When *Lloyd's List* reporter Tony Gray finally got through to him, Savarese admitted to being "bemused" by the confusion over the *Erika's* ownership, as if all the investigators ever had to do was to ask him. He told Gray that he had gone to France immediately after the accident and had spent five days there. He said, "No one was in hiding. I tried to be present at all the meetings that were taking place. But in a situation where you have a big tragedy like this, there are a million things going on at the same time." Furthermore, "No one tried to contact me, and it is not my job to contact the press." Gray had a sense of irony that his readers, particularly in London, must have appreciated. In deadpan prose he described Savarese's satisfaction that the *Erika* had been so well maintained that the crew had been able to lower the lifeboats despite the conditions at the time, and he repeated Savarese's admiration for the heroic acts of the French and British teams that had rescued the crew. About this ship that had just broken in half, Gray had Savarese saying, "There is no doubt about the good condition of the vessel." Savarese had proof too. He said, "I appointed a reputable management company (Panship), the vessel was classed by an IACS society (RINA), and had passed inspections by port state authorities and major oil companies . . . There is no doubt that everything was done according to the rules."

But that was precisely the problem, and as the *Erika's* filth continued to wash against the continental shores, even the general public was wising up to the realities at sea. Yes, over the previous two years the ship had successfully gone through four port state inspections—in the Netherlands, Norway, Russia, and Italy. And yes, its classification society, RINA, had given it even more thorough inspections and had declared it to be problem free. And yes, the ship's documents were in good order. And even, yes, Malta is a fine country with good hotels. But the truth was that the *Erika* was a decrepit ship, so badly corroded and poorly maintained that it had just broken up. Furthermore, the corrosion was a known problem that had plagued the ship for years. As far back as 1994 it had caused the *Erika* to fail a U.S. Coast Guard inspection in New Orleans, and since then of course it had only grown worse. It turned out now that the European inspectors had been aware of serious corrosion all along. What did it mean that the ship had still been operating within the law? It became obvious that rather than imposing high standards, the law had provided the necessary shelter for a liberated industry to do as it pleased. The structure of the new international order being promulgated by the IMO could be precisely calibrated by the corruption of the *Erika*'s steel.

Europe realized that the future had arrived, and it reacted much as the United States had a decade before, making explicit reference to the *Exxon Valdez* and to America's go-it-alone determination to defend its shores. Again the initiatives centered around the unilateral imposition of double hulls, though here too there was no reason to believe that a double-hull design (not inherently stronger than single-hull design and possibly more prone to corrosion) addressed the accident that had actually occurred. Europe was going to take action anyway, if only for symbolic effect. The French, who were the angriest just then, clearly understood the limitations of their geographic circumstances as compared to those of the United States. They realized that any imposition of new standards by France alone would have little effect on the parade of unsafe ships in the international waters off their shores, and would do economic damage to the country as the shipping industry shifted its trade to competing ports. The solution was regional action, specifically through the newly assertive executive branch of the European Union, the European Commission. Confident in the support of Europe's vast environmentalist constituency, the Commission's leaders took up the cause and proposed aggressive maritime reforms, including immediate double-hull requirements that leapfrogged over the American phase-out still in process. It seemed for several months that Europe was going to have its way—albeit by raising drawbridges and deflecting the disorder to other parts of the world, as the United States had done. This time, however, the IMO fought back: privately it accused the European Commission of technical ignorance and cheap political grandstanding, and in public it appealed to the high ideals of universal government. (Oddly, the United States joined in on the side of the IMO, deploring the regionalism of the European initiatives, a position greeted with bitterness by proponents of European coastal defense.) These arguments resonated, and by the end of 2000 the European Commission had essentially backed down. The shipping industry in return agreed to something like a false concession—an "accelerated" IMO phaseout of single-hull tankers, to be completed by 2015, though with loopholes and extensions that would allow many such ships to endure. There were some improvements in the application of port state controls. In the Netherlands, for instance, a ship-ranking system was put into place that forced the inspectors to board the most questionable vessels, rather than the newest ones, to achieve their quota of 25 percent; and in France it was now understood, almost as a cultural matter, that ship inspections had taken on the importance of national defense.

Southern Europe remained a problem, however. In the fall of 2002, while I was in La Coruña, Spain, exploring the aftermath of the *Kristal's* sad demise, I went aboard a Cyprus-flagged freighter that had just passed a Spanish inspection with not a single fault recorded. In reality this freighter was in such poor condition that its Georgian crew did not dare depart from the dock for fear that the ship would sink in the waves of the outer harbor. There were holes in the hull, flooded tanks, inoperative generators, and broken radios. The deck was so thin that it was possible to fall through. The owner, who was unknown, hadn't paid the crewmen for more than a month, and they were determined not to walk off the ship until he did. The catch was that he hadn't paid the dock fees either, and now the port was demanding that the ship give up its valuable space. In desperation the captain appealed to the representative of the seafarers' union, who, in my company, sought out the port inspectors and bullied them into rethinking their previous assessment and officially arresting what was obviously a dangerous ship.

The larger purpose of such an arrest was to deter such ships in the future from even approaching Europe's shores. This was the national policy as defined in Madrid, and it was the intent of the European Commission as well, whose leader in the fight against the IMO after the loss of the *Erika* was a Spanish official—an energetic and necessarily controversial woman named Loyola de Palacio. One might expect that in her activism she would have inspired the inspectors in La Coruña to do a better job. But the inspectors were soldiers on a front line, and there was reason to believe that they were discouraged and overwhelmed. Just a few weeks before, off the coast of Finisterre, a replay of the *Erika* had occurred as once again an old tanker had come apart in a storm.

This one was named the *Prestige*; it flew the Bahamian flag and had a Greek captain and a Filipino and Romanian crew. It was not a Spanish-bound ship, but was passing by in international waters, carrying seventy-seven thousand tons of industrial fuel oil in its hold, when it sprang a leak and began to list. The captain radioed for help and turned for La Coruña and the protection of its harbor. The Spanish authorities refused it shelter, and under the guns of their warships forced it to back out to sea. It was a cowardly act, a sign of governmental impotence and frustration. For five days the *Prestige* fought a losing fight offshore, wandering slowly, being battered to death by the storm. The crew was rescued. When finally the ship could endure no more, it did not simply bleed into La Coruña's harbor as it might have done, but broke in two and blew the filth of the world all over the coasts of Portugal, France, and Spain. In Finisterre now, people were marching in massive and angry demonstrations. They demanded that the government resign, and they sprayed signs on buildings reading NUNCA MAS! But this oil spill was really just a symptom. The inspectors, I imagined, were looking on with resignation, wondering how anyone could believe anymore that the chaos could be kept away.

Four

ON A CAPTIVE SEA

It is the extent of Western civilization—its success and apparent solidity—that magnifies the shock and terror on the occasions, however contained, of its collapse. On the oceans the most notorious such case in recent times occurred during the first hours of September 28, 1994, when the ferry ship *Estonia* foundered in the waves of a Baltic storm. The *Estonia* was a massive vessel, 510 feet long and nine decks high, with accommodations for up to two thousand people and a car deck that stretched from bow to stern through the hull's insides. It had labyrinths of cabins, a swimming pool and sauna, a duty-free store, a cinema, a casino, a video arcade, a conference center, three restaurants, and three bars. On the night of its demise, it had departed from its home port, Tallinn, capital of Estonia, and was proceeding on its regular fifteen-hour run, 258 miles west across open waters to the Swedish archipelago and Stockholm. Estonia at that time was a newborn nation of 1.4 million people, a coastal flatland nestled against the Russian border, near St. Petersburg. Merely three years before, in 1991, the country had emerged almost empty-handed from the ruins of the Soviet Union and had turned toward western Europe and the United States. Acquiring the ferry was part of that move. Through a typical arrangement of brass-plate companies, some based in Cyprus and Luxembourg, the ship was owned and operated by the Estonian government in full partnership with a publicly traded Swedish shipping company called Nordström & Thulin. Though the profitability of the Tallinn–Stockholm route was marginal, the ship was an immediate practical success, a link to the riches of the West, importing crowds of bargain-hunting tourists and traders and providing for a trickle of legitimate exports—and some smuggling too, mostly of people, weapons, and narcotics that were spilling out of the chaos in Russia. The smuggling allowed for payoffs to port officials and some of the crew, and it was generally accepted as an extension of a dynamic economy—an extreme of the new free-market thing.

The ship was a symbolic success as well. It was fourteen years old and had been purchased thirdhand, but it was freshly painted and white, and when at rest in Tallinn's harbor it dwarfed the grim gray buildings of the port and stood brightly for the promise of the new age. It had two sets of captains, officers, and crews, almost all of whom were Estonians. They worked two weeks on and two weeks off. People vied hard for those positions, and not only for the wages they provided. The *Estonia* was said to be the nation's pride. That was perhaps an overstatement, but there is no doubt that when the ship was lost, the collective trauma was severe. In Estonia nearly everyone knew someone who had disappeared, and even in Sweden a large part of the population was directly affected.

The shock was all the worse because the sinking had occurred on an ocean that people crossed casually, as if it were a captive sea, hemmed in by the civilizations that surrounded it, and therefore necessarily subdued. True, September was the start of the region's stormy season, but even the biggest storms there were small affairs compared to the gales of the open oceans, and the *Estonia* was a massive ship that seemed as if it could have sailed anywhere. As it happened, it had sunk so fast that there had barely been time to call for help. Something had gone monstrously wrong. Many people concluded that such a disaster could only have been the result of a deliberate act, and their belief grew stronger over the years. There was never good evidence to support it, but apparently it was easier to believe in perfect evil than to assimilate the complexities of accidental history.

The *Estonia* rolled onto its starboard side as it died. It lay in international waters, but not far from land, about fifty miles south of Finnish islands, among breaking waves and gale-force winds. There were other ships around. The sea was rough enough to have caused most of them to slow, but not so rough as to have caused concern. Then, in the middle of the night, a weak call was heard on VHF channel 16. "Mayday! Mayday! *Estonia*. Please . . ." A big Swedish ferry, the *Mariella* of the Viking Line, was nine miles to the northeast, and closest at the time. The chief mate was on watch. He thought he had heard the words "list" and "blackout," but he wasn't sure. He answered, "*Estonia, Mariella. Estonia, Mariella,* over . . ." The *Estonia* did not respond. It is known now that the man on the *Estonia*'s radio was the second officer, Tormi Ainsalu, and that he was on the bridge, bracing against a crazy tilt. Ainsalu was thirty-one and had been at sea for six years. Ignoring formal procedures, he called in the blind for another Swedish ferry normally in the area, the *Europa* of the

Silja Line. Desperately he said, "*Europa, Estonia! Silja Europa, Estonia!*"

The *Europa* answered, "*Estonia*, this is *Silja Europa* replying on channel 16."

Ainsalu said, "*Silja Europa!*"

"This is *Silja Europa* on channel 16."

Confusion reigned. Ainsalu said, "*Silja Europa! Viking! Estonia!*"

The *Mariella* cut in. "*Estonia, Estonia.*"

Ainsalu said, "Mayday! Mayday! *Silja Europa, Estonia!*"

The *Europa* said, "*Estonia, Silja Europa*, are you calling Mayday?" There was no answer. The *Europa* said, "*Estonia*, what's going on? Can you reply?"

Ainsalu apparently could not, but a new voice came on in his place. It was the *Estonia's* third officer, Andres Tammes, whose life was coming to an end at age twenty-eight but who had summoned impressive calm. Firmly he said, "This is *Estonia*. Who is there? *Silja Europa, Estonia.*"

"Yes, *Estonia*, this is *Silja Europa.*"

Tammes said, "Good morning." He had attended the Maritime School of Tallinn and had graduated from a Finnish maritime college two years before. He said, "Do you speak Finnish?"

The *Europa* said, "Yes, I speak Finnish."

Tammes said, "Yes, we have a problem here now, a bad list to the right side. I believe it is between twenty, thirty degrees." The list was already as much as twice that, but Tammes was fighting fear, standing his ground. Almost formally he said, "Could you come to our assistance and also ask Viking Line to come to our assistance?" He could not give the ship's position, presumably because he was hanging on to the high side near the bridge's port doorway and could not see the GPS indicator from there. He radioed that his inability to see was caused by a "blackout," though the ship's emergency power remained on and the GPS probably continued to function until the end. The *Europa* and the *Mariella* briefly discussed their uncertainty over where to proceed. Three minutes had elapsed since the initial distress call. Tammes asked for reassurance. He radioed, "Are you coming to our assistance?"

Europa answered, "Yes, we are. Can you tell me if you have an exact position?"

Tammes said, "I cannot say . . ."

Europa asked, "Can you see us?"

Tammes said, "Yes, I can hear you."

In desperation, the *Estonia*'s chief mate, a forty-year-old mariner named Juhan Herma, apparently slid or climbed down the deck to the GPS indicator—an act of bravery that undoubtedly saved lives but from which, for him, there would be no coming back. Five minutes after the initial call Tammes radioed, "I'll tell you our position now."

"Yes, go ahead."

As Tammes transmitted the coordinates, the chief mate could be heard in the background, shouting the information across the steeply sloping bridge. The ship had slewed uncontrollably to the east and was continuing its relentless roll. The captain was on the bridge as well, but was likely injured or dead. Passengers trapped below were screaming. The starboard wing of the bridge must have been very close to the waves. Tammes radioed, "Really bad. It looks really bad here now."

The *Europa* answered, "Yes, looks bad. We're on our way . . ."

The *Estonia* rolled onto its side, hesitated, and began to turn upside down. The ocean poured into the bridge, as it did into

every level of the ship. As the hull flooded, it began to slip below
the surface, stern first, at about a forty-five-degree angle, nose
high. Because the Baltic there was only about two hundred feet
deep, when the stern hit the bottom, the forward part of the ship
continued to protrude above the waves. From the helm of the
Mariella, which just then came onto the scene, the captain thought
the *Estonia* looked like a Christmas tree that had toppled, scattering its ornamental lights on the ground. Those lights were the lo-
cator beacons on rafts and rings, many of which were torn, flooded,
capsized, or empty. The Christmas tree blinked and went black
before it disappeared from radar. Where a luxurious ship had just
been, now there were only people in the water, some in rafts,
some trying to swim. Their cries for help could be heard above the
howling of the wind. The *Mariella* maneuvered gingerly among
them with searchlights on, rolling heavily, scattering life jackets
from its own supplies. Its sailors opened a fueling access door near
the waterline, hoping to drag in survivors, but almost immediately
had to close it because of high seas. For the same reason they
were unable to launch their rescue boats. Nonetheless, they managed to snag rafts containing fifteen survivors and to winch them
up the high sides to safety on board. Within two hours the *Europa*
and five other ships had arrived, and soon afterward they were
joined by four helicopters and then another four. The rescue operation continued through the dawn, concentrating primarily on
the rafts, and was rewarded with the last survivors around 9:00
a.m. Afterward, the math was all about subtraction.

It was a chaotic time ashore, with bodies arriving by helicopter
often naked and without identity, while frantic families clamored
for news and the international press roared toward the rescue operations center in the normally tranquil Finnish harbor town

of Turku. Not counting stowaways, the *Estonia* had been carrying 989 people, of whom 803 were registered passengers and 186 were crew. They included nationals of fourteen European countries—as well as Canada, Morocco, and Nigeria—but by overwhelming numbers they were Swedish or Estonian. Now the survivors were scattered among five rescue ships and in hospitals and hotels from Stockholm to Helsinki. In the confusion of the moment, the local authorities made some serious mistakes in accounting for them, particularly by listing a few of the missing as being alive—slipups that began almost immediately to feed conspiracists' fevers. When at last an accurate tally could be made, it became clear that merely 137 people had survived. That meant—incredibly—that at least 852 had died and, since only 95 bodies had been found, that most had gone down with the ship. Ignoring acts of war, what had just occurred was one of the worst maritime disasters in European history.

The casualties among the paying passengers were especially high, with 88 percent overall having perished, and 97 percent of the women. Physical strength had counted for a lot. Of fifteen children under the age of fifteen, only one had survived; and of 167 adults age sixty-five and older, every woman and all but two men had died. The survival rate among the crew was significantly better, 23 percent having lived, and this was later held against them, since maritime traditions might seem to require greater sacrifice in the face of such slaughter. The truth is that most of the crew consisted of service staff, with no definite role in an emergency and no particular nautical knowledge, and if their survival rate was relatively high, it was because they were disproportionately young and strong. Indeed, among the professional mariners aboard— the deck and engine personnel—the sacrifice was if anything too complete. The dead included the captain and the entire bridge watch, the chief engineer, and almost all the other officers and sailors on duty that night, as well as an entire cast of Swedish maritime experts, Nordström & Thulin's representatives, who had been aboard as technical advisers. Even the relief captain, who normally would have been off-duty and ashore, had come along for the ride because of a piloting exam he was scheduled to take the next morning in the Swedish archipelago, and he too had disappeared. Tragedy aside, once all such subtracting was done, there was no one left alive who was in a position to explain clearly and reliably what had gone wrong. This was an obstacle to understanding at the time, and to some degree it continues to be so today.

O n the afternoon of the accident, the prime ministers of Estonia, Sweden, and Finland established a board to look into the matter. The board was known as the Joint Accident Investigation Commission, or the JAIC. It was staffed in equal share by government officials and maritime experts from all three countries and chaired by the Estonian Minister of Transportation, a man named Andi Meister. Meister was an odd choice by investigative standards, since he had been closely involved in the day-to-day management of the ferry line. Indeed, the entire Estonian delegation, which had the primary responsibility here because it was their country's ship, seemed to consist of people sent forth to investigate themselves and their friends. In so small a society, such an arrangement was perhaps difficult to avoid, but it also bore traces of the old Soviet mentality, a tendency toward defensiveness and cover-up. The Swedish and Finnish investigators privately regretted the arrangement, which soon led to internal quarrels and began to impede their progress, but it was understood that for diplomatic reasons the board was to maintain a unified front. Estonia was to be treated respectfully, as if it were an equal nation, though of course it was not. This gave the Estonians power beyond their means, and it meant that the JAIC would have to produce a report that even the apparatchiks could agree on. But backroom bargaining over language and details is part of every important accident investigation worldwide, and in this case, among the frontline investigators—the Scandinavian mariners and naval architects who would be doing most of the work—there was never much doubt that the political obstacles could be overcome and that something like the absolute truth would be found.

The first indications were quick in coming. Within hours it was clear that reports from the survivors were all pointing in the same direction—toward the *Estonia's* bow. In dozens of short statements primarily to the Finnish and Swedish police, people indicated that the ride preceding the accident had been rough and fast, with pitching and violent slamming, and that it had finished with several massive metallic crashes that had caused the entire ship to shudder. The list to starboard had developed soon afterward, and it had rapidly become severe. Survivors described a capsize progressing so fast that most people had been trapped without a chance to reach the lifeboat deck, and crowds dressed in nightclothes or nothing at all had scrambled for their lives across the outside of the inverting hull. The speed of the capsize was an important clue, as were some negatives—the lack of fire or collision or any chance in those waters of having run aground. But the really convincing evidence had come at the end, as the ship was sinking inverted, stern first. Several of the survivors struggling in the breaking waves had looked up at the hull rearing overhead and had somehow found the presence of mind to notice that its front end seemed strangely square, as if the flared bow, the upper section above the keel's forward bulb, was simply no longer there.

To the investigators it seemed all too possible. The *Estonia* was a roll-on roll-off (or ro-ro) design, meaning that vehicles had drive-through access to the car deck, through openings and ramps at the stern and bow. Such access allowed for fast loading and unloading without the need for drivers to maneuver or back up. The car deck stood just above the waterline. Access to it through the stern posed no particular problem: when the ship arrived in port and backed in to berth stern first, twin steel ramps—like drawbridges or tailgates hinged at the bottom—could be lowered hydraulically to span the gap to the pier. When the loading was finished and the stern ramps were raised again, they nestled hard against their frames, forming an integral and watertight section of the outer hull. At the front of the car deck, access to the ship through the bow was a trickier affair. There was a ramp there too, also hinged at the bottom and hydraulically operated, which functioned like a forward-facing drawbridge that could be lowered to the pier when the ship berthed nose first. This bow ramp, when raised into its vertical "closed" position and locked against its frame, formed a watertight bulkhead much as the stern ramps did. But in that position, rather than being part of the outer hull (as similar ramps are on the squared-off bows of military landing craft), it was enclosed by an additional outer shell, in the form of a pointed, classically shaped ship's bow. This presented the obvious problem that before the bow ramp could be lowered, somehow the outer shell, the bow itself, had to be gotten out of the way. The solution aboard the *Estonia*, as on most ferries, was to build the upper bow section as a movable "visor"—hinged at the top on the outside foredeck—that could be hydraulically raised and tilted back out of the way, much as the highly articulated hood of a car might be. Because the entire opening—from bow visor to forward ramp to car deck—stood above the waterline (if barely), there was no danger to the ship in port. Before the ship proceeded to sea, however, it was essential that the forward ramp be raised and clamped into its watertight frame and that the bow visor be lowered and locked firmly into place. Such double protection was necessary when the ship was under way, because even in flat seas, the bow wave rose higher against the hull than the level of the car deck, and in heavy weather it rose higher still, at times burying the entire nose in masses of green water. In such conditions the forces were enormous, and they were directed primarily upward, the direction in which the hinged bow visor, by design, was naturally inclined to lift and open. This created inherent vulnerabilities that the ship's builder needed to take into account, as did its regulators, owners, and crews. Should the double protection (the wave-proof bow and the watertight loading ramp) somehow fail, even minor flooding on the car deck could threaten the entire ship, owing to what is known as the free-surface effect: the large, uninterrupted parking expanse would have allowed the water to slosh and accumulate on one side or the other, where because of the car deck's elevated location in the hull (two levels above the keel), the weight could have a disastrous effect on the ship's stability.

The danger was known to the entire industry, and of course to the JAIC investigators: water merely knee-high on the car deck could cause such a ship to turn over. Seven years before, in 1987, a British ferry by the subsequently awkward name *Herald of Free Enterprise* had capsized immediately after departing from a

Belgian harbor in calm weather; the crew had mistakenly left the bow door open, and more than 150 people had died. In the aftermath, the IMO made some typically minor changes in international standards, intended to improve flooded stability of roll-on roll-off ferries, but they were applied to new ships only (at best), not to existing vessels like the *Estonia*, which had been built seven years before the British loss. It seemed obvious that the same error had not been committed here, because the *Estonia* had proceeded through half the night and against large waves before foundering. But if indeed the bow visor was missing from the hull, its absence would go far toward explaining what had gone wrong.

On September 29, the day after the accident, a Finnish survey ship towing a side-scan sonar set out to find the sunken ship. Its search was hampered by the heavy seas and confused by uncertain coordinates, but on the second day, it discovered the wreck (at 59°22.9' north, 21°41.0' east) and marked it with a buoy. The ship was still lying on its starboard side, partially inverted at an angle of about 120 degrees, pointing eastward from where it had come, on a down-sloping bed of soft clay. A debris field lay behind it, to the west. The sonar image of the bow was inconclusive, but the Finns returned, and during the two weeks that followed, they used unmanned submersibles known as remotely operated vehicles to examine those parts of the ship's exterior that could be seen—almost everything except for its starboard side, which lay buried in the muck. During the work, several cameras failed, causing gaps in the individual records, and some edits were perhaps made to prevent gruesome images of the dead from being released to the public. These gaps later gave critics the chance to push their claim that the Finns were involved in a cover-up (for reasons that had to be imagined), but in truth the photographic record as a whole was complete, and it showed that the hull was undamaged except at the nose, where the forward loading ramp was hanging partially open and the bow visor had been torn off and had disappeared without a trace.

The question now was, why? The bow visor was found about a mile to the west, and it was eventually salvaged and taken to a Finnish port. The Swedish government hired a Norwegian deep-water diving company to survey the wreck in greater detail. Two months after the loss, the company sent down a team of specialized divers. With visibility limited to a few feet in the dark and murky water, the divers penetrated the car deck and also explored the inverted bridge and a few cabins, where they encountered the dead, some floating alone, some in clusters. They brought up key components and steel samples that they cut from hinges and latches at the bow, as well as a few navigational items and the ship's bell. The diving company had been asked to assess the possibility of raising the hull, and it concluded that this could be done, though with difficulty, and with additional complications because of the human remains still trapped inside. The Swedes waffled but ultimately decided against the salvage, largely because they believed it would serve little practical purpose. Logically, then, they also decided against removing the dead, and they announced that the Estonia's victims had effectively been buried at sea. The wreck, in other words, had become a permanent gravesite and was not to be disturbed.

These decisions were answered by loud objections, most noticeably from some families of the dead who had organized into disparate groups, many claiming to speak on behalf of all. Sweden stuck to the policy anyway and sought to strengthen it by criminalizing unauthorized intrusions into the Estonia—by underwater filmmakers, treasure hunters, thrill seekers, historians, voyeurs, conspiracists, or any of the others who constitute the global sub-culture of wreck divers. The legal ploy was weak, however, since the *Estonia* lay in international waters, beyond Swedish enforcement powers. Furthermore, wreck divers tend to be physically aggressive and independent-minded types for whom such a restriction might only add to the appeal. Indeed, the uninvited did dive to the *Estonia*, some brazenly, and when they got there, they stripped items from the ruins and no doubt gazed irreverently through the portholes at the figures of the dead. In frustration Sweden embarked on an unusual attempt to protect the site by entombing the entire ship in concrete, and it went so far as to dump several loads of gravel onto the wreck before abandoning what in retrospect was an impractical and predictably contentious idea. It later turned out that the *Estonia* had shifted under the debris, as if rolling with indignity in its grave. This caused a whole new round of bitterness. And it was sad, because the Swedes who had rained stone into the Baltic were not criminals, as some people claimed, but rather quite the opposite—they were well-intentioned regulators, squeamish about the death of so many innocent citizens and frustrated by their inability to impose order on the scene.

Meanwhile, the JAIC was struggling with its own emotions, mostly internal, which were related to the Estonians' different worldview, their sly obstructionism, and the looming need to assign relative fault for the accident. There was never much question that the bow visor had come off and that the ship's second line of defense, its forward loading ramp, had opened up as well. But because of the differing agendas, more than three years were required to show how and why this had happened. It was boring work mostly. It involved sifting through the ship's routine records and piecing together hundreds of witness testimonies, some of which were revealing but many of which were not. The most important evidence was physical or photographic, ultimately reduced to laboratory reports of the numbing kind, replete with color close-ups of torn and bent steel, superimposed arrows pointing to relevant features, with rulers to provide scale—documents that even the engineers had to struggle to get through. The investigation grew more interesting when the evidence allowed the JAIC to begin reconstructing the events and to test the hypotheses against mathematical models to see if they made sense. Of particular importance were the waves that night, the forces on the bow, the sequence of structural failures, and the progression of the capsize.

If anything, the process got too interesting then, and politics intruded. Andi Meister was forced to step down as JAIC chairman and to resign from his position as Estonia's Minister of Transportation in order to keep disputes from breaking into the open. The head of the Swedish delegation had to resign as well, in the midst of an artificial scandal that in any other context would have been shrugged off as a minor thing. One Swedish and one Finnish investigator died, each of natural causes, and most others came to wish they had never gotten involved. Increasingly, as it became clear that the commission was concentrating on the *Estonia's* design, its members came under orchestrated personal attacks, primarily for their motives—a particularly vicious sort of accusation because it purported to read their minds and allowed them little self-defense. For millions of northern Europeans, who naturally did not pay close attention to the details, the tale of the *Estonia* was tainted, and if only through association, so was the investigation. The JAIC might have paid more attention to these image problems, but it was inherently ill-equipped to handle them, in part because there were indeed problems with the Estonians' role. In Stockholm and Helsinki, where good work was being done in detail, the technical investigators responded ineffectually by hunkering down with their science.

In December 1997 the final report came out. At its core it found that the *Estonia* had been maintained and operated correctly according to international and national regulations, and that the bow visor had failed (and fallen off) because its attachment points to the hull (hinges and locks) had been grossly inadequate to withstand the forces imposed on them by ordinary storm waves. The ship had survived for so many years under its original Finnish owners only because it had operated in sheltered waters, among the Finnish and Swedish islands across the entrance to the Gulf of Bothnia. In other words, these weaknesses had accompanied the ship since birth, and they had caused the bow to fail quite predictably within a storm season or two on the new open-water run. To make matters worse, the bow was not visible from the normal positions on the bridge, so when the visor came open and began initially to swing up and down, the officers on duty had no idea this was happening, and they neither turned nor slowed the ship. As for the collapse of the second line of defense, the supposedly watertight bow ramp, the report described another catastrophic problem with the design. Because of the way the top of the ramp nestled inside the visor, the two systems were not truly independent, as they should have been, and the failure of one led inevitably to the failure of the other. Simply put, as the bow visor broke off, it knocked the ramp down too. After that, the ship kept sailing ahead with its mouth wide open, gulping up the sea.

The report tried to be fair. It stated that at the time the *Estonia* was built, no unified international standards for such designs existed. But it also stated that there were private standards known to be in use that would have made the ship stronger, that in any case it should have been obvious that this bow arrangement was inadequate, that the builders' handwritten strength calculations were "simplistic," and that the ship as built was even weaker than its design. The report apportioned some responsibility to Bureau Veritas, the French classification society that had contracted to certify and monitor the ship during its construction and throughout its life, and to the various Baltic maritime administrations which, by relying too heavily on the French and not disseminating information on previous bow-visor failures, had failed to protect the public. Primarily, though, the report laid the blame on the doorstep of the ship's German builders—a family-owned shipyard named Meyer Werft. These were the people, it said, whose inadequate design and shoddy construction had led to so many deaths.

As might be expected, the report was controversial, and it remains in dispute today. Though the investigators presented good evidence to support their conclusions, they signaled their largest weakness on the very first page, when they asserted categorically that the report was "unanimous on all points." Anyone aware of the complexities of the accident, or of the makeup of the JAIC, knew that such a statement could not fundamentally be true. Moreover, the Meyers were a proud family, and they were determined not to take the fall.

For more than two hundred years they had run their yard on the river Ems, in Papenburg, on Germany's North Sea coast, surviving the successive crises of European history and spawning oceangoing vessels that included sailing ships, modern cruise liners, and ferries. (In 1914 Meyer Werft built the colonial East African steamer *Graf von Goetzen*, which later had a brief film

career hunting Humphrey Bogart in *The African Queen*, and today, despite being twice sunk, continues as the Tanzanian Railways ferry *Liemba* on Lake Tanganyika.) The Meyers had at first
cooperated forthrightly with the JAIC, but quite early on, as the
inquiry turned in their direction, they had understood the need
for self-defense.

The family is understandably private about its affairs, and the
details of its inner workings are not known, but the story as it
played out conjures up images of worried stakeholders gathering
in a wood-paneled study to hear from company director Bernard
Meyer about the risk to their shipyard. The situation was clearly
very serious: this was not the case of some freighter dragging down
an anonymous Third World crew, or even of a tanker spilling oil,
but of a passenger ship killing hundreds of modern, middle-class
Europeans—people who lived a half century removed from hard-
ship and took it as a birthright not to die such deaths. Thank God
there had been no Americans on board, litigious as they are. But
the Estonians were up to Soviet-style tricks, and the Scandinavians seemed to be caving in. It is impossible to know whether
deep within the family the stakeholders wondered whether their
yard had indeed built an unsafe ship. In practice, such thoughts
would have been irrelevant anyway. There was really no choice.
The family was at war.

They brought in a hired gun to do the job. He was a senior attorney in Hamburg named Peter Holtappels, who already was a
trusted associate of the yard. Holtappels stated for the record
that Bernard Meyer had asked him to put together a group of
technical experts to investigate the true cause of the accident, and
that he, Holtappels, had agreed to lead the effort only on condition that the inquiry would be completely independent, free

from Meyer Werft's interference—though Meyer Werft was to fund it. In light of the group's subsequent work, this reads like an inside joke, an ironic reference to the JAIC's own claim to independence. Holtappels understood the mission perfectly well, and over the years that followed, he executed it with relentless precision. It amounted to a flanking maneuver, by which a band of consultants—led by Holtappels and dubbed the "German Group of Experts"—not only matched the progress of the JAIC but attempted to go beyond it and, through sheer volume of alternative evidence and interpretations, to surround and overwhelm the official report's conclusions. Along the way, Holtappels picked up allies among the families of the dead, who added a moral if somewhat confused presence to his campaign, and through the device of weeklong "exhibitions" in Stockholm, where emotions ran strongest, he got the interest of the press. Predictably, the point being made was that the ship was solid by design, but poorly maintained and brutally handled—and furthermore that all this was so obvious that the JAIC must have known it, and was engaged therefore in a cover-up. Meyer Werft, in other words, was yet another victim. The second of the exhibitions was timed to coincide, in December 1997, with the publication of the JAIC's final report. Members of the JAIC were invited to attend, and of course they did not.

The JAIC disbanded, leaving a few lonely alumni to defend its conclusions on their own. As a result, Holtappels and his German Group wandered the field for another two years almost unopposed. In the spring of 2000 they published their own final report, and eventually posted it on the Internet. It was a convoluted document, many thousands of pages long, that dwarfed the JAIC's more focused product, and it seemed to contain every tangent that Holtappels's people had pursued. Its contents ranged wildly from rumors and sly personal attacks to elaborate constructions of genuine evidence, good reasoning, and scientific fact. The report was difficult to read and assimilate in its entirety, and though it contained some strong points, it was weakened overall by leaps in logic and unsupported assertions, as well as by being quite obviously self-serving. But no matter—Holtappels was a practical man. He had not been hired to build a unified argument here, or to demonstrate his intellectual elegance, and what he had produced was a weapon all the more effective for its breadth and weight. It was never quite able to overturn the JAIC's conclusions, but it succeeded in creating plenty of confusion and doubt about them, a fog that lingers on. Whatever the real reasons for the *Estonia's* loss, Holtappels performed a miracle of damage control, and Meyer Werft emerged from the catastrophe with its reputation and finances intact.

The collateral effects have been widespread. Among them is the rise of the hard-core conspiracists who, never prone to shyness, circled the accident from the start but nourished themselves heavily on the German Group's work and used it to gain the kind of fluency with details that can sound like deep knowledge. The connection was natural, since Holtappels's report suggested that the JAIC was a cover-up—which itself would have been an epic conspiracy, requiring the cooperation of hundreds of people from three separate countries with mutually distinct interests in the case. But the true believers went further still, insisting that the JAIC was just a rearguard action and that the *Estonia* had been sunk intentionally in a plot that involved Russia, Estonia, Finland, Sweden, and of course the puppet master itself, the United States. It would have been laughable were it not taken seriously, but in a Europe where full-blown conspiracy thinking thrives—particularly in Germany, where for instance one-fifth of the public (and a third of those under thirty) now believe that the U.S. government was behind the attack on the World Trade Center—the conspiracists gained a large following. And their existence turns out to have mattered, largely for the distraction they created and the inaction that resulted, with consequences for passenger ship design that will endure until perhaps the next maritime disaster.

Out of curiosity, therefore, I went to Potsdam, near Berlin, in the fall of 2003, to meet the former German television reporter turned filmmaker who has led the conspiracist crusade. She is a middle-aged woman named Jutta Rabe—blond, aggressive, stocky—who descended on Finland on the morning of the accident and has stayed with the story ever since. She interviewed survivors and families of the dead, reported on the JAIC's progress, attended Holtappels's Stockholm exhibitions, and became convinced rather early that the *Estonia* could not simply have gone down in a storm. She believed that the ship had been bombed and that a great injustice had been done. Her company is called Top Story Productions. She runs it with a man she calls her life's partner. They produce investigative documentaries and television dramas, usually shot in English because the market is larger and Germans are accustomed to seeing movies that have been dubbed. We talked in her office at an exciting time, with phones ringing frequently and congratulations flooding in, the week before their first feature film was to open in three hundred theaters throughout Germany. It was *Baltic Storm*, a political thriller about the *Estonia* and Rabe's quest for the truth, based on her book by the same name. I had read the book. She told me that it was a best seller in Germany, that it had been translated into Estonian, Swedish, and Finnish, and that it was ready in a revised second edition to hit the North American market—preferably tied to a major movie distribution deal, yet to be found. She seemed very confident. She mentioned that over the years as an investigative journalist, she had made fourteen documentaries, of varying lengths, about the *Estonia*. She said that for the current film the story had been slimmed down and some of the characters fictionalized, but on the important matters pertaining to the crime and the cover-up, it presented the absolute truth.

In the building next door, in a small, comfortable screening room, I sat through a showing with a couple of working critics and a group of invited guests, mostly friends or family of the cast, who were so well attuned to the story already that they reacted to the JAIC characters as if on cue, with scornful little laughs. The film had cost about $17 million to make, a third of which had come from the German state. It was filmed in English, in a docudrama style meant to educate and persuade, and it opened with a line that read, "Any resemblance to certain events is purely intentional." An introductory segment included shots of the fall of the Berlin Wall, and of various presidents, including Bill Clinton, under whose regime the *Estonia* had disappeared. The writer and director was an American named Reuben Leder, a Hollywood pro with a background in American television that clearly showed. The stars included veteran British actress Greta Scacchi, playing a glamorized Rabe character, as well as Jürgen Prochnow, once such a fine German U-boat commander in *Das Boot* but awkward here in the sentimental role of an *Estonia* survivor who has lost his son. Donald Sutherland drops in for a few scenes as a Pentagon official reeking of special knowledge and self-satisfaction. It was all a little embarrassing, but the film was a genuine artifact in the struggle for possession of the *Estonia*'s history.

The core of the story was familiar to me from Rabe's earlier works of reportage. Rogue elements in Russia had sold a secret weapon to the Pentagon and were getting it to the United States by smuggling it to Stockholm in a truck on the ferry. A Russian scientist with a briefcase full of sensitive documents was along for the ride. To keep the deal from going through, former KGB agents boarded the ship, and shot the scientist, the captain, and a sailor on the car deck. Then they placed charges against the bow door locks and the hull, detonated them, and escaped in a lifeboat. Afterward, the Swedes, Finns, and Estonians caved in to an American-led cover-up so intense that it included the need to "disappear" the ship's relief captain, who had survived but somehow knew too much. In reality, the relief captain was among those who had been erroneously listed as alive in the confusion of the first hours, but such errors were simply not believable to the conspiracists, who had a curiously admiring view of governmental competence. Indeed, Rabe had concluded that the others erroneously listed had been made to disappear too, precisely because they had been in a life raft with the relief captain and knew therefore that he was alive. That particular twist was too much for the movie script, which smoothed it out of existence and for the sake of satisfaction had Rabe's surrogate find her way onto a secret American base, where she discovered the relief captain in a bewildered state with a surgical scar across the back of his skull.

Rabe in real life was never able to make such a discovery. As described in her book, she fell repeatedly short of finding the sort of hard evidence that once and for all could have proved her theories. The closest she came was a diving expedition on the wreck that she mounted in August 2000, provoking deep anger and a warrant for her arrest by the Swedish government, whose declared

gravesite she was openly violating. Rabe scoffed at their sensibili-
ties. Her purpose was not to disturb the dead, but to find and film
proof of the villainy that she knew had put them there—a bomb
hole in the hull, below what had once been the waterline. The
divers did not find such a hole, however, and they returned to the
surface with a video image, inconclusive at best, of a dark spot
along the mud line, where the ship was resting on its starboard
side, and some clearer pictures of torn steel from the visor attach
points at the bow—old news unless it could be shown that the
damage was due to explosives and not the force of the sea. For
that reason Rabe's divers salvaged samples of the steel, which
eventually made their way to reputable metallurgical laboratories
in Germany and the United States, where they were examined for
microscopic signs of a bomb blast. In all but one case the results
came back negative. The exception was with one of two samples
examined by Southwest Research Laboratories in San Antonio,
Texas, which reported back cautiously that certain aspects of the
steel (called "twinning" and "necking") could be considered evidence of "shock loading," but that this could not be confirmed because of extensive corrosion. Additional experiments were needed,
the report said, in which the sample in question would be compared to new control samples "generated under known conditions."

This was hardly the result that Rabe had been looking for, and
though she asserted publicly that it constituted positive proof of a
bomb blast, she never followed up on it or had the sample tested
again. The dive in practice had failed her, but rather than giving
her pause, it seemed to have reinforced her perception of a world
submitting—through incompetence, gullibility, cowardice, corruption—to the shadowy political forces in control. In August
2001 she mounted another expedition, and this time only placed a
banner on the wreck. It read:

IN MEMORY
of more than 850 innocent
victims, never forgotten by
the people but abandoned
by their countries
Sweden, Finland, Estonia
hiding the truth and
refusing to find the guilty.

It was a strange thing that had happened to her. She was an energetic, well-intentioned person, the daughter of a Hamburg shipyard worker, and therefore she felt an affinity for the ocean. She had gone off to university in Berlin and for years afterward had worked as an investigative journalist, uncovering the news in places as distant as China. From personal experience she must have known the size of the world. Apparently, however, she had trouble imagining the extent of the sea. It probably didn't help that the Baltic on a map or from an airplane seems small and contained. In her book Rabe downplayed the size of the waves that the *Estonia* had encountered, and by the time the movie came along, the ship seemed to be cruising across a surface that was generally calm. For whatever reason, and if only in this one case, Rabe refused to accept the confusions of history, and she grew angry at others who more easily did. They became dupes in her view, or worse, they became complicit. She was not paranoid, as some conspiracists are, but she had long been engaged in a mentally tricky profession, uncovering little truths hidden away from view, and she had slipped now into a pit from which escape was difficult. The latest result was this movie. It was a feeble drama but an interesting product of the mind. After the screening, one of the critics came up to me and said that he hadn't quite understood the plot. Had I? I shrugged. An explanation would have required too many leaps. And it was not plot that mattered here as much as purpose. Rabe told me that her intent was to reach a larger audience than she had reached before. That was her pragmatic side. But she was also using the movie as a way of bringing order to a disorderly place—the ocean at night where a failing ship foundered in a storm. On film, a sort of civilization could at last be forced into view, if only by getting Donald Sutherland to emerge from a helicopter and confess.

Five

THE OCEAN'S WAY

There was civilization on the *Estonia* for real, until the ocean seized control. The ship left Tallinn only fifteen or thirty minutes late, and for the first several hours, as dusk turned to night, it moved through sheltered coastal waters, striving to catch up with its schedule. Those on deck would have seen gray forested islands creeping by to the north, and to the south, the long, industrial shoreline of Tallinn giving way to a low coast, darkening as it faded into the night. Gentle swells rolled in from the west, indicating the sea's unease, but their significance was probably apparent only to the crew, who had received storm warnings for the open ocean ahead but had not spread the news. There were various forecasts, and they tended to agree: an intense low-pressure system near Oslo was moving quickly to the east and was expected to drag rain and strong winds across the route, stirring up waves occasionally as high as twenty feet. Such conditions were rare for the area, occurring only a few times every fall and winter, but for ferries of this size they were not considered severe. Surviving crew members later claimed that a special effort was made on the car deck to lash the trucks down securely—exemplary behavior which, if it occurred, probably had more to do with concern about vehicle damage claims than concern for the safety of the ship. No other preparations were made. The crew's main concern was to arrive in Stockholm on time, at 9:00 the following morning.

As evidenced by their subsequent handling of the ship, the captain and his deck officers considered the *Estonia* to be seaworthy and stout. Moreover, they had fresh paperwork to prove it. That very afternoon in Tallinn a group of Estonian shipping inspectors, receiving on-the-job training from a couple of their Swedish counterparts, had performed an extensive port state control inspection of the ship, and in the end, using a crudely modified Swedish form, they had submitted a list of only minor discrepancies, essentially giving the *Estonia* high grades for its condition. The Swedish instructors were less impressed, and later stated for the record that they had noticed a disconcerting lack of respect for issues related to seaworthiness—hatches left open on the car deck, worn rubber seals on the bow visor, a certain nonchalance by some of the deck officers—but nothing that could have justified detaining the ship in port. Safety came first, of course. But off the record, it was inconceivable anyway that the Estonians would permit a group of port inspectors to interfere with this symbol of national progress. In the minds of sailors, port inspectors are mere bureaucrats in disguise. And once at sea, the *Estonia* was run as if nature itself had no right to slow it down.

That night the ship knifed ahead at 19 knots, with all four main engines fully throttled up to their combined output of 23,500 horsepower, driving the hull relentlessly into the accumulating seas. The vessel's motion was at first barely noticeable to the passengers. Inside the *Estonia*, the public spaces had the look of a coastal casino designed around a nautical theme—completely serviceable, but overdecorated in red, a bit worn, a tad out of date. Though many couples and a few groups were aboard, collectively it was a ship full of strangers with little time to get acquainted or, as people do on longer passages, to fall even temporarily in love. The experience of the sinking therefore turned out to be lonely and highly atomized. Observers who later claimed that a social breakdown had occurred failed to take that into account.

Still, at first that night there was something of a cruise ship atmosphere on board, as passengers dropped their bags in the cramped Pullman-style cabins and emerged to explore the possibilities for whiling away the hours. Their choices ranged from lingering in the sauna and pool on Deck 0, deep below the waterline, to visiting the various bars, entertainment spots, and restaurants on Decks 4, 5, and 6. Deck 7 contained the crew cabins, but it had an outside promenade for passengers who wanted to feel the wind and watch the ocean surge by. An external staircase led to additional outside space on Deck 8, from which the lifeboats hung on davits. Because of the wind and the cold, only a handful of the hardiest passengers ventured outside. The others lingered over their drinks and meals, and as the evening drew on, they talked, read, gambled, or watched dancing girls and listened to Estonian rock in the big Baltic Bar, on Deck 6. The singer there was a genuine talent named Urmas Alender, who, until being forced into exile by the KGB, had been the lead vocalist for a politically potent Estonian band named Ruja, which for nearly two decades had stood for resistance to Russians and their language. This job on the ferry must have been understood as a sign that Alender, at age thirty-nine, was past his professional prime. But he was still a famous man, and probably the best-known person to die that night.

By 10:00 p.m. the *Estonia* passed north of a lighthouse called Osmussaar and was moving through the open ocean in deteriorating weather, with rain, strong winds, and an overcast scudding low and fast across steep seas. The ship had nearly caught up to its schedule and was still running at full power, but it was slowed inevitably now to 17 knots by the impacts of the waves, which rose regularly to ten feet and higher. Sheets of salt water were torn loose by the plunging and driving of the bow. They swept as heavy spray across the foredeck and rained against the forward cabin windows as high as the upper decks. The winds came from the left, off the port bow, and gave the *Estonia* a permanent list of several degrees to starboard. The list could not be prevented, because the ship had left Tallinn slightly out of balance, and the port-side heeling tank had already been filled in compensation. However, this was not considered to be a problem and was too slight to be noticed by the passengers. Though the motions of the hull were complex, the ride was rough mostly in pitch and not in roll, because the waves, unlike the winds, came from nearly straight ahead. The ship heaved upward and vibrated in the heaviest water, and slammed down into the troughs, sometimes with a crash. The motions were difficult to predict even for the crew.

Some passengers grew seasick and retired to their cabins to suffer in private. This was not the best tactic, since the cabins were tiny, and most of them were located forward in the ship, where the motion was most violent. Just getting to them would have been a trial for the nauseated. The interior hallways of the accommodation sections were windowless fluorescent-lit passageways smelling of aluminum and plastic, barely wide enough for two people to pass. They ran fore and aft, with branches from side to side. With their bright twenty-four-hour illumination and long rows of anonymous, closely spaced cabin doors, they gave those parts of the ship an institutional allure not much different from that of modern prison galleries.

Farther back, in the public spaces, the ship's motion was calmer, and the ride remained comfortable enough for the more stalwart passengers. They continued to dine in the restaurants and to sit around in the bars, drinking and enjoying the entertainment. Here was Urmas Alender himself, singing songs in Estonian that already seemed nostalgic—reminders of a recent past, when national solidarity could be expressed only in such code, and of the speed with which life had changed. Outside, the storm kept growing stronger. A few glasses fell and shattered. Eventually the dancing girls began to stumble. Thirty minutes past midnight, Alender stopped singing because of the ride, though he was scheduled to perform until 2:00 a.m. People remained in the bar anyway, drinking. Eleven bodies would eventually be found there by the Norwegian divers brought in by the JAIC, but that was two months ahead, in an invisible future.

Up on the bridge, which straddled the ship one level above Deck 8, the officers standing watch were apparently not inclined to slow down. Hardly anything is known about their conversation, and though presumably it touched on the weather, there is no evidence that they were worried. The bridge was darkened for night vision, but little was visible outside. The waves were black masses, the foam a dim white. Occasionally the ocean spray rose so high that it pelted the windows. Slowly the *Estonia* overtook the lights of other westbound ferries and passed them by. At regular intervals the captain showed up to check on the progress. He was an experienced mariner, Soviet trained, named Arvo Andresson, who at age forty had a heavy face with sideburns about ten years out of date. On several of his visits he was accompanied by his friend Avo Phit, the relief captain, who would make his final appearance in Jutta Rabe's film as the tragically sympathetic victim of American brain surgery. In reality, both men were known to the *Estonia's* crew as authoritarians in the Soviet maritime style, little interested in the initiatives of subordinates, unwilling to brook dissent. Captain Andresson was diligent, however, and announced that he would be available, on call, until 5:00 a.m., when Phit would take over in preparation for his piloting exam, during which he would guide the ship through the Swedish archipelago. Andresson expressed concern not directly about the weather, but about the continuing loss of speed and its effect on the schedule. One of the men on the bridge who heard his comments was a trainee second officer named Einar Kukk, who was supposed to be learning his duties by observing on this, the queen of the fleet, before transferring to a lesser ferry on the Tallinn–Helsinki run. Kukk survived. He later remembered that around 11:00 p.m. an especially large breaker reared up out of the darkness and hit the ship hard on the left side of the bow. This may have been the wave that caused the glasses in the bar to fall and break. Captain Andresson was not on the bridge at the time, but he appeared about thirty minutes later and stayed for a quarter of an hour. During his visit he asked the third officer if all four engines were in operation, apparently to verify that the ship was maintaining its best possible speed. The third officer assured him that they were.

About then, a Polish ship named the *Amber* passed by in the opposite direction, having an easier ride because it was heading down-weather for Helsinki. Years later, Holtappels's German Group (gunning hard for Andresson) tracked down the *Amber's* first mate, who had been standing watch and remembered the crossing. According to the German Group, the first mate said, "The ferry was brightly illuminated, and appeared to proceed against wind and sea at full speed, which I could hardly believe. . . . She was pitching heavily, and I saw how she was taking a lot of water on the forecastle deck which smashed against the superstructure and was thrown up to the bridge windows, and spray was all over the vessel. When her bow smashed into the waves I had the impression that she almost stopped, and subsequently built up speed again when the foreship rose. In my opinion, those in charge on the bridge of the *Estonia* must have been crazy, absolutely incompetent and inexperienced. I had never seen anything like this before." The mate's testimony sounds at once too detailed and hyperbolic to be reliable, and it contains a contradiction, impossible to resolve for a ship of the *Estonia*'s mass, between nearly stopping with each impact and immediately afterward achieving the full cruising speed that Andresson could only have wished for. Nonetheless, there is no doubt that the *Estonia* as it fought forward into the gale must have made for an impressive sight.

By then it was known on the bridge that many of the passengers felt sick—a consideration, however frustrating, that generally causes ferry captains to slow their ships long before concern about hull strength comes into play. Rigid though he was, Andresson was not immune to the problem. The ship was rolling more heavily than it had before, compounding the discomfort caused by the head seas, and it was due to turn 25 degrees to the right at a navigational waypoint ahead, after which, with waves then coming from farther to the left, the rolling could be expected to increase beyond tolerable limits. Andresson therefore gave orders for the ship's roll stabilizers to be activated at the turn point. The stabilizers were hydraulically powered retractable fins, like stubby wings, that extended, one per side, from pockets in the hull below the waterline. They rotated in contradiction to the ship's natural rolls, relying on dynamic pressures caused by the forward progress through the water, moving in opposite direction to one another (one up, one down) much as ailerons do on airplanes. Because of drag, their use would entail a further loss of speed. Having decided on that sacrifice, Captain Andresson left the bridge at 11:45, as the trainee Kukk remembered the time. By midnight the waves were rising to twenty feet and the winds to 50 mph—conditions that matched the worst of the forecast, and were continuing to degrade. Twenty-five minutes later the ship came to the waypoint and altered course to the right as planned. After a delay caused by the brief failure of the starboard fin to extend, the roll-stabilization system was engaged, and the speed dropped to 14 knots, with all four engines still running hard. The ride remained very rough. For Kukk it had been a long night. He finally left the bridge, and after a stop at a karaoke bar on Deck 5, the Pub Admiral, he retreated to his cabin, which was one level lower. It was nearly 1:00 a.m. He needed a rest, and he undressed, but as it happened, he lacked the time to sleep.

With Kukk's departure from the bridge, uncertainties deepen about the *Estonia's* final moments. Among all the mariners on the bridge that night, only one other man survived, and he turned out to be a defensive and unreliable witness. He was a twenty-four-year-old named Silver Linde, a simple sailor whose duties included serving as a lookout when he was on the bridge and walking through the ship once an hour on the half hour, on thirty-minute safety rounds. Whether out of intimidation at having to face questioners or genuine concern about his role during the foundering, after the accident he was visibly worried about saying the wrong thing. He gave conflicting testimonies that in detail seemed sometimes to be fabricated as well as confused. Whatever the reason, he proved incapable of providing the type of coherent technical narrative that the Scandinavian investigators hoped for when they rushed to question him in Turku the day after the accident. However, he did provide glimpses. Linde said that he had started his last regular safety round on schedule, about thirty minutes past midnight, and he implied that he had not been worried about the worsening storm. In fact, his safety round was at first a bit of a lark: he lingered with friends on Decks 8 and 7 and then stopped by the Baltic Bar on Deck 6 to look for a woman who worked there; when he didn't spot her, he went downstairs to the Pub Admiral to check for another woman, who likewise was gone. The trainee Kukk saw him there briefly in an employee doorway. Dutifully, then, Linde proceeded with his round, descending in the central stairwell casing to the car deck (Deck 2), where he emerged after opening one of the sliding fire doors.

From this point on, Linde's story has been hotly disputed by Holtappels's group. According to Linde, the car deck was dry. He walked forward toward the ramp, bracing himself against the bulkheads to maintain his balance until, when he was nearly at the front, the ship slammed upward into a wave with a huge metallic-sounding crash. The motion was so violent that Linde nearly fell. He used his walkie-talkie to report the sound to the second officer on the bridge, who instructed him to investigate. Linde checked diligently and waited around for about five minutes, but he saw nothing unusual and heard no further crashes, and so after continuing his round by descending to Decks 1 and 0 (or not, depending on his testimony), he climbed the stairways through the superstructure, checked again at the Baltic Bar, and returned to the bridge, arriving just behind Captain Andresson, who stepped through the door at 1:00 a.m.

Jutta Rabe or her partner later asked Linde, "What happened on the bridge at one o'clock?"

Linde answered, "No, no," apparently to deny an implication. Then he said, "Everything was in order. Nobody was worried."

But Captain Andresson had not shown up merely by chance. To the second officer he said, "What's going on?" The second officer informed him that there had been calls, presumably from crew in the hotel staff, that strange crashes could be heard coming from the area of the bow. Andresson's response is not known. It is now widely believed, and generally accepted by Holtappels's group as well as by the JAIC, that the crashes were the sound of the suddenly unsecured bow visor smashing up and down in the largest of the waves and preparing to break entirely free. The crew on the bridge must not have known this. The bow visor was not itself visible to them, but according to Linde, a short flagpole (for pennants) attached to the bow could be seen, and it was in a normal position. Andresson did not order any speed reduction or sheltering turn. The second officer asked Linde to go back to the car deck and see what was happening. Linde left the bridge after a stay of only a few minutes.

The confusion thickens. According to the last of Linde's testimonies, before proceeding to the lower decks, he checked once again for his friend at the Baltic Bar. At about that time, the ship assumed a slight but noticeable list to starboard. Linde seems to have understood at last that something was very wrong. He hurried to the information desk on Deck 5, either to inform the hostess there of possible trouble (as he stated once) or to ask her to unlock the car-deck doors (as he stated at other times). Possibly both are true, or neither. Either way, when Linde got to the information desk, he had to wait, he said, because the hostess was busy exchanging currencies for a passenger. It was then, at roughly 1:15 a.m., that the *Estonia* was hit with two heavy impacts felt throughout the ship. Linde did not mention those impacts, though they were extraordinarily violent and loud.

According to Jutta Rabe, plastic explosives had just been detonated. They had been set against the bow mechanisms as well as against the hull, down below the waterline on the starboard side. And the weather wasn't actually as bad as it was officially said to have been.

According to the JAIC, the entire bow visor had just sheared off, for reasons relating to the weakness of its attachments and the power of the sea. It had smashed the vehicle ramp open, and had struck and dented the bulbous bow on the port side while falling free.

According to Holtappels's group, various explanations exist, ranging from bombs to the incompetence of Estonians, but one thing for sure is that the work of Meyer Werft, a good German shipbuilder, had nothing to do with it.

Everyone agrees that immediately after the heavy impacts, the ship wallowed briefly from side to side, and then heeled over so far to starboard that objects began to fall. Apparently Linde never did talk to the hostess at the information desk. He headed down to Deck 4. By the time he got there, the heel was about 15 degrees, and the entrance foyer was full of passengers struggling toward the stairways—many of them undressed and in terror. Some shouted that there was water on Deck 1. The hostess got on the public-address system and in a thin and frightened voice said,

"*Häire! Häire! Laeval on häire!*"—Estonian for, "Alarm! Alarm! There is alarm on the ship!" It was a nonstandard alarm, spoken in a language that was incomprehensible to hundreds of the people aboard, but it was the only clear verbal warning that many of the passengers ever received. Down on Deck 4, Linde could not move against the surging crowd. He turned around and climbed the stairs to Deck 7, but he fell while heading up the sloping floor toward the outside promenade on the port side. Lying there with passengers struggling by, he radioed to the bridge that people were shouting about water on Deck 1. He was heard by others on the frequency to report flooding on the car deck as well, though at a confusion of different times. An officer on the bridge ordered him to descend again and assess the danger. Already it was a hopeless task—and indeed it would have been a suicide mission. By then Linde had managed somehow to gain the outside promenade. He then lost his radio in the chaos of the crowd.

Deep in the engine and machinery spaces that filled the aft half of Decks 0 and 1 below the waterline, three men were on duty that night, all of whom survived. They included the third engineer, who was in command, a system engineer who had been called in to handle a plumbing problem, and a motorman, whose job was essentially that of mechanic's assistant. The third engineer's workstation was the control room, a brightly lit place with arrays of panels and switches that had windows overlooking the engine room proper and was insulated from the roar of the machinery there. It was a world apart from the storm outside, though of course it rolled and rocked, and occasionally it shook when large waves hit the bow.

The control room was equipped with a video monitor showing critical areas of the ship, including the forward end of the car deck and the nestled bow ramp. Linde appeared there on the monitor during his final safety round. The third engineer observed him on the screen, and though he was uncertain of the time, he agreed that the ramp seemed secure then and the car deck looked dry. Around 1:15, however, he felt the powerful blows on the hull, and when he checked the monitor again, he saw water gushing violently around the edges of the ramp and pouring onto the car deck. As he remembered it later, Linde came onto the radio right away with a report of the flooding. The third engineer had the instruments to measure the effects: the ship rolled 3 degrees to starboard, 1.5 degrees to port, then rolled back to starboard and stayed there. Within about two minutes the list had grown steep. The system engineer and motorman came rushing in and witnessed the terrifying scenes on the screen. The motorman in particular was badly frightened. Later he remembered seeing waves rolling through at cartop level.

By now the officers on the bridge had throttled back the engines and had begun to turn the ship to the left, perhaps out of concern that a right turn would have exposed the high side of the hull to the wind and waves, increasing the starboard list. The effect of the turn, however, was to swing the open bow directly through the oncoming waves, which probably worsened the flooding. One of the bridge officers called down to the third engineer and asked him if he could counter the list by filling the port-side heeling tank. He could not, because the tank was already filled, but he tried desperately to pump in additional ballast water in the hope that the list might have created additional space. It had not, and the third engineer abandoned the attempt. Objects were falling in the control room; it was impossible to stand without holding on.

At about 1:20 the bridge issued a muddled and coded alarm over the public-address system, "Mr. Skylight one and two," which interpreted literally was a call to fire stations, including one on the flooded car deck. Some of the crew concluded that the ship was on fire and tried to get to their muster stations, but movement was very difficult. The JAIC investigators later had their own interpretation of the "Mr. Skylight" message. Because it was a limited alarm, they took it to mean that the officers on the bridge did not yet fully grasp the trouble they were in. The ship continued turning·left and slowed to about 5 knots. It was still proceeding under power. But as the list exceeded 30 degrees, the oil pressure dropped, and the four main engines automatically cut off—engines one and two on the port side first, followed by engines four and three. Under the weight of the floodwater, the ship settled visibly lower into the seas. By 1:22 the bridge officers seem to have understood that the ship was going down. The lifeboat alarm sounded—seven short horn blasts, followed by a long one—and bells began ringing throughout the ship. Simultaneously, up on the bridge, the second officer, Tormi Ainsalu, broadcast the first weak call for help on VHF channel 16. "Mayday! Mayday! *Estonia.* Please . . ." The auxiliary engines were still running, providing power to the ship. The watertight doors dividing Decks 0 and 1 into compartments had been closed. The idea was to prevent the sort of sequential flooding that took the *Titanic* down, of relevance particularly should the ship be punctured below the waterline. The compartments were capped by the watertight car-deck floor, but they were open to the superstructure above through stairwells and elevator shafts that rose through the car-deck level inside the long, narrow (and supposedly watertight) sheath of the central casing. For the moment, the engine compartment remained dry.

In the control room, the third engineer used railings to crawl to a master panel, where he struggled in vain to restart the main engines. He released the motorman and system engineer. They opened a hatch and began to climb an emergency escape ladder that led to the top of the ship through the inside of the funnel. For strong men it turned out to be negotiable at nearly any angle. The list by then was 45 degrees and increasing rapidly. Before the two men reached the top, the auxiliary engines cut off. After a brief pause in blackness, an emergency electrical generator on Deck 8 automatically started up. The officer on the bridge called down again to the third engineer and asked him if he could empty the freshwater tanks on the starboard side. The third engineer answered that he lacked sufficient power. Vehicles could be heard shifting and banging on the car deck. The time was 1:30 a.m. The ship was pointed to the southeast and was drifting eastward at 1.7 knots. As high as Deck 8 on the starboard side, windows in the public spaces of the superstructure aft were breaking under water pressure and the pounding of the waves; and one level higher, the bridge itself was reaching for the sea. As the list passed 60 degrees, the third engineer ducked through the emergency hatch and climbed for his life in a funnel that would soon be horizontal.

Earlier that evening, by about 11:00 p.m., the restaurants had closed and most people had retired however queasily to their cabins. In the Baltic Bar on Deck 6, a Swedish passenger named Pierre Thiger lingered over an Irish coffee, enjoying the show. Thiger was a Stockholm-based ship broker, age thirty-two, who had gone to Estonia to look over a small freighter and was travel-

ing home alone. This was his fourth trip on the ferry, and the
roughest he had experienced on any vessel. As something of a
mariner himself, he believed that the ship was being driven too
hard, but he was not particularly worried. Earlier in the evening,
he had run across an acquaintance in the crowd, and the two men
had dined together before proceeding to the bar; now they listened to Urmas Alender good-naturedly, without caring about his
songs or knowing who he was. As the weather grew rougher, the
waiters had trouble moving between the chairs with their trays,
and a speaker on wheels began to roll back and forth on the stage.
At one point a dancing girl fell into the band. After Alender called
things off at 12:30, Thiger and his friend headed down one deck
to the Pub Admiral, where the festivities were still going strong.

The Pub Admiral was aft of midship on the starboard side.
There were perhaps fifty people there. The entertainer was a
Swedish musician named Pierre Isaksson, who in the 1960s and
1970s had belonged to a popular quartet called The Family Four,
but now belonged to the ferry company and was visibly farther
along than Alender on the downside of a musical career. He was
leading the crowd in songs. The audience was loud and drunk.
The sound system was turned too high. Both of the eventual survivors from the bridge—Silver Linde and the trainee Kukk—
briefly stopped by. Thiger and his friend sat at the back of the pub
at first, but then moved forward for a better view and perched on
two high stools near the stage. Neither man ordered a drink.
Thiger liked to sing, and he joined Isaksson for a song, then took
his seat again. The two men knew each other from previous voy-
ages, and they commented that they shared the same first name.
Several other passengers joined Isaksson to sing. At Isaksson's
urgings, the crowd sang too. Just before 1:00, when the show was

scheduled to end, the entertainer, as Thiger later remembered, said, "We have such an amusing time tonight, so I think I should extend the time a little."

It was soon afterward that Thiger heard the metallic-sounding blow that reverberated sharply through the ship's structure. At first he thought it must have been caused by a heavy wave, but it didn't quite feel like ordinary "slamming." He wondered if a truck might have overturned on the car deck, but no, the impact was too strong for that—it was almost as if a whiplash had run through the bulkheads. Thiger did not express these thoughts, and his friend said nothing either. A murmur may have rippled through the crowd, but the noise level was too high to tell for sure; the mood was determinedly festive. Thiger heard a clear comment from only one passenger, a man nearby who joked, "Ha! Now we have sailed against an iceberg!" and took another gulp of beer. The singing continued unabated. About half a minute later another impact was felt, identical to the first, and Thiger got the distinct impression that the ship was swerving. He said to his friend, "Do you feel it? We are swinging longitudinally now." His friend said, "Yes, we are." Thiger felt a little unsettled, and he reassured himself with the thought that the ship must have turned directly into the waves, perhaps to lessen the rolls while the crew lashed vehicles or cargo more securely to the decks. Suddenly, however, the ship shook with a strange back-and-forth movement and began to wallow. It rolled to port and starboard a few times, then rolled steeply to starboard and came back a little, but never returned to level. The initial list was enough to cause glasses to come crashing off a shelf and for a speaker to roll across the floor and crash.

The music stopped.

Thiger felt butterflies in his stomach. To his acquaintance he said, "Now there is something completely wrong. Let's get out of here."

"Yes, as you say," his acquaintance said.

The two men jumped up, but they had taken only a few steps toward the exit when the heel increased to an angle that Thiger estimated to be about 30 degrees. There was immediate panic in the pub, with much shouting. The bar counter stood along a wall on the pub's port side. The bartender had braced herself behind it, but she collapsed screaming under a deluge of bottles and glasses. Refrigerators came loose, and stools slipped out from under patrons, who clung to the countertop to keep from falling. Others were not so lucky. They slid across the floor in a confusion of tumbling tables, chairs, and sound equipment, and they piled up in tangles along the ship's starboard side, down-deck from the exit. Then the bar counter itself broke loose. Many people were injured and subsequently died. It is not clear where Pierre Isaksson was. Pierre Thiger and his acquaintance managed somehow not to fall. But movement across the pub's open spaces toward the exit was now extremely difficult, even for such agile and sober men.

At the receiving side of the Pub Admiral's deadly collapse, along the starboard wall just across from the doorway to the ship's interior halls, sat another Swede of about the same age, a recreational diver named Rolf Sörman, who turned out to have prodigious reserves of calm and great presence of mind. Sörman wore a gold chain around his neck. He was a member of a small human resources group that was making a round-trip from Stockholm in order to hold a shipboard seminar in the *Estonia's* aft conference room—an alternative to holding the seminar in a hotel, and a common practice on Baltic ferries. As a young man, Sörman had toyed with the idea of going to sea, and he had spent some weeks as an officer in training on a Swedish ferry of the Silja Line before deciding that law school would provide for a better life. Like Thiger, he disapproved of the speed with which the *Estonia* was being driven into the waves, and he contrasted this handling, as he later said to me, with the policies he remembered from the Silja Line, in which the ships were slowed early for passenger comfort, in the expectation particularly that people would maintain their spending in the restaurants and bars. These Estonians were evidently not quite ready for such capitalist subtleties. Earlier in the evening, Sörman had watched as they pushed their ship brutishly past the *Viking Mariella*. At dinner, many of the people in his seminar group were sick. They had a preordered three-course meal nonetheless, and three bottles of wine for their group of twelve. Afterward they broke up for the night, but Sörman and four of the women headed up to the windward promenade on Deck 7, port side, to look at the sea. When they got there, the doors to the outside were swinging open and shut, apparently because a latch had broken, and the carpet leading from the stairwell was soaked with saltwater spray. Three of the four women grew nervous about going outside.

Eventually they all found shelter in the Pub Admiral. They ordered beers, and for a while sat too close to the speakers to be able to talk. Well before 1:00 a.m. they retreated from the noise to the farthest reaches of the pub, which happened to be across from the exit, along the ship's starboard wall. During that short walk, Sörman felt two or three distinct shocks on the deck under his feet. These appear not to have been the heavy blows felt by Thiger and others. There was time afterward for leisurely conversation. The women sat on a sofa that was bolted to the floor. Sörman sat facing them on a chair. There were windows in the

wall, black with the ocean night. Five minutes before 1:00 a.m.,
over Sörman's affable objections, one of the women excused herself. Her name was Anita Person-Flygare. She walked forward past
the information desk, up the main staircase, and directly to her
cabin on Deck 6. When shortly thereafter the ship heeled over, her
door popped open and she fell backward in her cabin, pinned by
gravity against the far wall. Because she was determined and nimble, she managed to emerge from the trap, to negotiate the tilting
hallway, to climb to Deck 7 and the outside promenade, and ultimately to survive.

Rolf Sörman and his three remaining companions moved even
faster. As the Pub Admiral collapsed into chaos, they jumped onto
the sofa to avoid the sliding debris. A wave lapped against the windows beside them, then covered the glass with solid green water
lit by the light of the ship's interior. When the ship rocked back
from the steepest angle, Sörman and his group seized the opportunity to gain the exit doorway nearby. They waited there briefly
for another cycle, then lunged across an open space and dashed
through a lateral corridor toward the aft stairway, which was near
the center of the ship on the port side. During that dash a falling
refrigerator nearly hit Sörman and then smashed into a wall. A
man emerged from a forward corridor shouting, "Don't panic.
The crew has everything under control!" Sörman and his companions were not panicking. On the other hand, they believed that
the ship was out of control. They came to the aft stairway. Using
the railings and brass banisters, they hauled themselves rapidly up
two levels, encountering only a few other passengers along the way.
They did not hear the weak and impromptu, *"Häire! Häire! Laeval
on häire!"* At the top of the stairway, on Deck 7, they found that
some of the crew (whose cabins occupied that deck) had formed a

human chain to help people up the sloping floor to the promenade doors. When the ship heeled more steeply, however, the crew disappeared to the open deck outside. Sörman and his group made it to the doorway nonetheless, and by grasping the frame, they pulled themselves through. They were among the first passengers to reach the promenade. After failing to open one of the lifevest boxes, they succeeded in opening another. Still functioning as a group at that time, they helped one another to find complete life vests with no missing straps, and to put those life vests on.

Pierre Thiger and his acquaintance were slower to escape from the Pub Admiral, though not for want of trying. The brief opportunities provided by the rolling motion—the cyclical moderations of the starboard heel that Rolf Sörman had exploited— were spoiled for them by the distance to the exit and the presence of other passengers ahead who were either too shocked or too drunk to move quickly or get out of the way. Afterward the floor angles grew so steep that even full-body crawling was ineffective. Here again, though, people formed human chains. Thiger and his acquaintance were able to reach the hallway outside. With the further use of human chains, they struggled across the ship amid scenes of bedlam and fear, and arrived at the aft stairway. By then the stairway was choked with fleeing passengers, many of whom were hanging on to the railings as if paralyzed. Thiger and his acquaintance tore loose their hands and shouted in their ears to get them moving, and after an agonizingly slow climb they finally arrived on Deck 7, somehow negotiated the steepening floor, and moved through the double doors to temporary safety outside. They were among the last to make it there. Since the first catastrophic heel, maybe eight minutes had gone by. The list had increased by now to 40 degrees. When it got to 45 degrees two or three minutes later, escape from the ship's interior was no longer possible, except for the engine-room crew.

Survival that night was a very tight race, and savagely simple. People who started early and moved fast had some chance of winning. People who started late or hesitated for any reason had no chance at all. Action paid. Contemplation did not. The mere act of getting dressed was enough to condemn people to death, and although many of those who escaped to the water succumbed to the cold, most of the winners endured the ordeal completely naked or in their underwear. In any event, the survivors all seem to have grasped the nature of this race, the first stage of which involved getting to the Deck 7 promenade without delay. There was no God to turn to for mercy. There was no government to provide order. Civilization was ancient history, Europe a faint and faraway place. Inside the ship, as the heel increased, even the most primitive social organization, the human chain, crumbled apart. Love only slowed people down. A pitiless clock was running. The ocean was completely in control.

Oddly enough, the relative distance that people had to travel seems to have made little difference. In the crew cabins on Deck 7, whose windows gave directly onto the port-side promenade, divers later spotted the bodies of twelve victims who had gone down with the ship. Conversely, the passengers with the longest escape route fared surprisingly well. These were the occupants of the ship's claustrophobic basement—the cramped economy section that filled the forward half of Deck 1, below the car deck and waterline. Because of their proximity to the bow, these passengers turned out to have a double advantage: first, an uncomfortable ride kept many of them awake; and second, they had an early warning in the form of strange, watery noises and metallic crashes that aroused their curiosity and concern for half an hour before the bow fell off. This combination helps explain why the hands-down winner of the entire race came from Deck 1. She was a Swedish woman, age thirty, who expressed concern to her companions at the onset of the unusual sounds and climbed the stairs fully clothed to Deck 7, where she arrived quite calmly and took a seat at least fifteen minutes in advance of the terrified crowds.

When the bow fell off, it made a screech and a howl, and it hit the port side of the hull so hard that some people in the forward cabins were thrown out of bed or against the walls. Down on Deck 1, passengers who were already well primed to run sprang immediately into action. Up and down the hallways, doors popped open and people emerged. As the leaders fled, they saw water in various forms—running in rivulets on the floor, rushing like a river, spurting from wall fittings, or cascading down from overhead. Their escape routes led up six short stairways to a common passageway inside the car deck's center casing, from which separate stairways then led upward, primarily to the *Estonia*'s large entrance foyer, which spanned the ship at the base of its main staircase on Deck 4. The center casing was still mostly dry, but floodwaters sprayed the fleeing passengers through gaps around the car-deck access doors.

Those left behind had a hard time. From what little is known about conditions on Deck 1, panic broke out when the windowless world began to turn onto its side. The shouting there was very loud. People were trapped in their cabins, either too weak or too injured to overcome the increasing list. In one doorway a tough old woman hung on determinedly, trying to pull herself out. People ran back and forth in the main hallway, colliding with one another in uncertainty about where to go. Movement soon became difficult. As the angle increased, many who had found their way to the stairs realized that they lacked the arm strength to keep climbing. One woman dressed in a nightgown stood at the base of the stairs screaming hysterically. Others who had stalled partway up seemed passive and resigned. They were passed by people who could not help them and who, although still capable of movement, were themselves losing the race to escape.

On the upper passenger decks—4, 5, and 6—in the extensive accommodation sections, the hallway scenes were just as rough. People who had emerged from their cabins were trying to escape along the fore–aft corridors, whose regulation width of 3.9 feet ultimately became their height as the ferry rotated onto its side, forcing the herds of people who were starting to walk on the walls to crouch as they attempted to proceed. Some of the crew were seen trying at enormous personal sacrifice to help them along, but all was terror, congestion, and noise. The starboard cabin doors were traps that had to be jumped across. Passengers who failed fell into the cabins, and some did not emerge. The transverse corridors became dangerous shafts that dropped away to the starboard side and, once seawater began to enter through breaking windows, became deadly wells. A particularly vicious trap was an apparent escape route at the forward end of the superstructure, a small stairway that led upward through the stacked accommodation sections from Deck 4 all the way to Deck 7 on the ship's high port side. It could be reached on each deck only by crossing the forwardmost of the transverse corridors, but before the list grew too steep, some quick-thinking passengers succeeded. These were people who should have survived, and a few of those who were ultrafast did, but there was a catch with this route, and it was lethal. The principal stairways on the ship were built in a fore–aft direction—an orientation that allowed them to be scaled (by strong people, using the railing) at relatively steep angles of heel. This little stairway, by contrast, was built in a transverse direction—side to side—a detail that meant that as the list increased, the stairs went vertical and then inverted, cutting off the possibility even of retreat. Months later, divers found so many bodies there that they could not get through to take a complete count.

Most of the passengers fled toward the main staircase at the center of the ship, emerging into the large open spaces that surrounded it on every deck, and then crawling or lunging as best they could to gain the banisters and railings. The trainee officer Einar Kukk rushed through at an early stage, on his way to Deck 7, and he later reported that the handrails gave way from the start. As more people arrived and the list increased, passengers began to slide and fall, and some were crushed by toppling equipment. The scenes of loss and bedlam defied coherent description by the survivors who witnessed them. On Deck 4, two women who had gained the staircase lost their grip and fell fatally against a wall. Others had already been badly injured, and some were lying apparently dead. Emotions among those unable to climb varied widely, with some people screaming incoherently, others seemingly listless and confused, and still others rational, self-contained, and brave. One of the survivors, a young man who had been trying to guide his parents and his girlfriend to safety, got separated from them in the chaos while gaining the stairs. When he looked back to find them, it was obvious that they would be incapable of negotiating the open space, across which increasing numbers of people were fatally sliding. They shouted at him to save himself. It was practical advice. There was no time to linger over the decision. He turned and continued on alone.

On the higher decks, hundreds of similar tragedies unfolded

as the gathering crowds struggled upward and people exhausted their strength against the ever more difficult heel. The main stairways were choked with passengers and a few of the crew. Those no longer capable of movement clung to the railings or sat on the landings, just waiting for the end. People fell onto each other. One woman lost her husband to another woman that way. Among married couples the strong were delayed by the weak. It is evident from the rarity of single spouses among the survivors that many couples decided consciously to die together. These were not the sad, sweet moments one sees in the movies. There was no music. There was the strange announcement, "Mr. Skylight, one and two," which was difficult to hear over the screaming. On every level the view from the main stairways was of carnage and confusion. People lay in the mouths of the hallways, unable to figure a way across the open spaces. It is not known what happened to the hostess at the information desk on Deck 5, except that she did not survive. One female crew member and then another slid with a scream across the foyer, hit a wall, and grew silent. Presumably, they too died. From the stairway, some of the survivors saw a row of gambling machines fall onto passengers emerging from near the shops. The injured seem to have begged for help, but conditions simply did not allow the witnesses on the stairways to intervene. The calculation was instinctive. To release one's grip on the railings for even a moment now was to fall, and to fall was to perish.

Up on Deck 7, at the top of the main stairways, a few extraordinary men—both passengers and crew—were trying at great risk to themselves to help people emerging from the climb to get through the double doors to the high port-side promenade. People who failed to catch the door frame slid on the carpeted deck and were killed or injured, or they ended up on the starboard promenade, on the low side, from which they were washed into the sea early as the ship continued to topple. At least one of them survived. In any case, the race to freedom was nearing an end. At some point someone secured a rope to the port-side promenade and dangled it down into the stairway. It was found in the wreck by divers, and it probably came too late, since none of the survivors mentioned its use. The last known attempt on the doorway was made by a woman who lay hanging on to the threshold before losing her grip and sliding away.

At the rear of the ship on Deck 5, in a café called Neptunus that adjoined the Pub Admiral, the ocean was flooding into the starboard side. A man there had been fighting hard to save his mother. He had removed his shoes and socks for a better grip, and he was dragging his mother upslope by bracing against the tables, which were mounted on pillars and bolted solidly to the floor. The two had managed to stay out of the encroaching water and, with periods of rest, had struggled to within two tables of a port-side door that gave onto an open deck at the stern. At that point his mother lost the last of her strength, and announced that she could go no farther. She was paralyzed not by fear or lack of will, but by a simple physical fact: no matter what her mind said, her muscles would not perform. This was a reality her son now needed to understand. She lay on the floor, hanging on to a table, the ocean lapping up at her from behind, and she insisted that he leave her. At first he refused and shouted at her to keep going. But she could not, and as his mother, she ultimately prevailed. He disappeared through the door, and after crossing the stern deck, he found railings and fixtures that let him scale the ship's outside structure at angles of heel that by then were too steep to allow escape for even the strongest of the nearly seven hundred people left inside.

The promenade decks, port and starboard, were lined with life-vest bins and cradles holding heavy life-raft canisters, and they were overhung by large fiberglass lifeboats suspended from davits—ten in total, five per side. Between difficulties caused by the angle of heel and the lack of coordinated action by the crew, none of the boats would be lowered, although nine would break loose when the *Estonia* finally sank, and they would float to the surface as flotsam—damaged, overturned, swamped. For now, as the list steepened, the starboard promenade spilled ominously toward the reach of the waves, and the port promenade did the opposite, rising and tilting upward until its floor and the recessed exterior wall of the Deck 7 housing, between them, formed a perfectly balanced right-angle V open to the sky. Though initially the V stood on the ship's protected downwind side, as the capsize continued, the promenade grew increasingly exposed to the wind and spray by the diminishing inclination of the sheltering wall. The wall rose only one level, to the open, rooflike expanse of Deck 8. It became a floor when the starboard list increased beyond 45 degrees, and the *Estonia* lay fully down to die. But even such imperfect shelter was preferable to the horror inside, and nearly all of the escapees took refuge there, on the port promenade. In total there were perhaps two hundred and fifty people. Some of the crew struggled individually to live up to the responsibility that had been vested in them. The relief captain, Avo Phit (destined to become Jutta Rabe's celluloid martyr), was last seen trying to rally his troops; the trainee Kukk was busy with the lifesaving equipment, and even Silver Linde, having lost his radio, acquitted himself well. The situation nonetheless was beyond salvation, and the chaos on the promenade was intense. The collective screams of the victims trapped below rose through the stairwells like a cacophony from hell, a protest that for those on the outside near the doors it drowned out even the roar of the storm.

Some of the escapees panicked, crawling around on the promenade and adding their own screams to those below, or begging hysterically for life vests, or sitting apathetically against the walls, or rushing to and fro without purpose, like terrified creatures losing the last ground in a flood. Such hopeless or incoherent people, however, turned out to be the exception. Despite the unusual danger that confronted them on the ship's outsides, most of the escapees seemed to keep their wits about them and to remain effective even at severe angles of heel. A brutal selection was at play, by which those who had succeeded in gaining the promenade tended by definition to be precisely the sort of people who could best handle the threat that awaited them there. They were fast and strong, and capable of quick calculation. Though their actions once outside were largely self-centered, with personal survival predominating over other concerns, many of them proved capable of working together to achieve that end—preparing and deploying the heavy life rafts, for instance, or attempting to free the lifeboats, however impossible that turned out to be. A few went further. One man in particular comes to mind. He stood on the promenade looking completely composed, reassuring passengers around him that they would survive, patiently instructing people on how to don the life vests, and setting up an efficient system for the vests' distribution. It was as if human society, having been torn apart, was starting to remake itself already—as if with time there could have been kings and queens on that drifting hull, and maybe even priests. But then the ocean washed them all away.

There was criminality too, perhaps because among the various admirable characteristics being selected for, the less admirable traits of opportunism and raw aggression lay inextricably entwined. Indeed, some of the first people to follow Rolf Sörman and his three female companions outside onto the nearly empty promenade were brazen thieves—a band of young Estonian men who took advantage of the confusion to tear the gold chain off Sörman's neck and to strip the cash and jewelry from the women. With startling speed they robbed others on the deck and then disappeared inside, apparently to work through the crowds that were just beginning to surge up the staircases. They were confident, as criminals tend to be, and they must not even have considered that the ship might then trap them, though the best evidence is that it did.

Sörman was angered by the assault. Still, preoccupied with finding adequate life vests for himself and the three women, he was soon confronted with aggression of a more dangerous kind. The problem started as fighting that broke out among passengers competing for life in the aft stairwell—violent behavior related to panic, but more focused and productive, that had the effect of intensifying the selection process under way and, especially toward the end, of delivering onto the port promenade predators who had managed to come from behind and would stop at nothing to survive. A group of these people emerged from the aft stairwell as the list approached the cutoff of 45 degrees, and, having fought their way to the promenade, they lunged at passengers already there, wresting life vests from their grasp or tearing them off their backs. People fought back, of course, but some lost. It is not known what happened to the victims, but if they went into the water without flotation gear, as some passengers did, it is fair to say that they were murdered. The effect of the fighting on Sörman and his companions was less direct, but serious enough. They were separated into two pairs, with the fighting in between—two women on one side, Sörman and the third woman on the other—and because of the risk of being attacked, they were unable to join up again. The women on the far side disappeared, and did not survive.

Sörman's sole companion now was a middle-aged Swede named Yvonne Bernevall, who had participated in the seminar with him but was not a close friend. Like Sörman, she was physically strong. To escape from the aggressors on the promenade, the two of them clambered up to the open expanse of Deck 8. It was quieter there. The deck (which, again, constituted much of the ship's roof) was like a steel beach angling dangerously down toward the oncoming waves. Its slopes however were covered by nonskid rubberized mats, and were interrupted by life-raft cradles, pipes and protuberances of various kinds, and the walls of higher structures, including most notably those of the captain's quarters and the navigation bridge above it, and of the large midship funnel—all of which allowed for adequate purchase. As the hull continued to capsize and flood, it grew heavy with water, and its movements softened, with the unfortunate effect that the waves reached higher against the decks, plucking off victims in small groups, or one by one. When the auxiliary engines failed and the lights flickered off, a new round of screaming erupted, but it settled again when the emergency generator kicked in. Increasing numbers of people arrived on Deck 8 (actually now climbing *down* to it) because the formerly upward V formed by the promenade had rotated so far to the starboard that the alternative escape route, across its rails and onto the ship's port side, had risen beyond their reach.

The storm was howling. The ship was visibly sinking by the stern. Already the aft starboard corner of Deck 8 had gone under. Passengers and crew deploying the automatically inflating life rafts were having trouble with the wind, which blew unsecured rafts entirely away and jammed others against railings and edges. The wastage was enormous. The ship had safety equipment for more than two thousand people, but it was clear that among the few hundred escapees outside, many would go wanting. Desperation mounted. Getting the rafts into the water, and then getting into them, proved to be just about impossible. Most rafts when activated turned out to be underinflated anyway. The good ones were too few to keep up with demand. On Deck 8 an apparently perfect raft suddenly inflated—the full thing, complete with a raised tentlike canopy and a little flashing light—and in response, a large crowd rushed it, far too many people to get in. Yvonne Bernevall wanted to rush it too, but Sörman was afraid of the crowd, no less for its mood than for its size, and he persuaded her to stay away. He had no intention of going into the water. From his experience diving in the tropics, where even in tepid waters he had to wear wet suits to stay warm, he was convinced that he would die very quickly of the cold. But he was struggling with a life-raft container of their own, and he had hopes of getting it open in time.

When the list was 80 degrees, as loud crashes came from inside the ship, a hatch popped open in the funnel and Sörman saw the terrified motorman emerge from his climb. The motorman started shouting in English, "Water is coming in on the car deck!" until the system engineer, having emerged beside him, smashed him in the face to calm him down. They disappeared together. The third engineer must have emerged soon afterward, though he was not seen by Sörman. The bridge windows were now breaking in the waves. The rubberized mats were coming off the decks, piling up in jumbles, falling onto swimmers in the water. Then the funnel touched the ocean's surface, marking a list of 90 degrees, and a cloud of acrid steam enveloped the ship as the seawater contacted the hot exhaust pipes inside. The electric generator failed, and people screamed, but the batteries kicked in, illuminating fluorescent emergency lights. A rocket flare arced into the night. The ship's horn blew a loud and mournful good-bye. The hull began to invert. Faced suddenly with the prospect of the ship rolling over on top of them, scores of people still hanging on to Deck 8 began to drop into the water and attempt to swim clear. They were on the dangerous upwind, up-storm side. Some got tangled in wires and cranes, or were dragged down or killed by the impact of the waves. At midship the heaviest waves crashed nearly to the top of the deck, and aft they surged entirely over it. Sörman had to abandon his hopes for the life raft in the container. He had no faith in his life vest to keep him alive. He sought the hand of Yvonne Bernevall for her company, and together they fell into the sea.

Pierre Thiger took the alternate route to the water that night, as did about half of the people on the promenade. When the deck's angle reached 45 degrees and the promenade took the form of a perfectly balanced V, he climbed outboard over the rail and perched outside of it on an edge above the ship's port-side surface expanse—the window-lined superstructure immediately beneath him and the heavy steel hull farther below. Though the storm was growing worse, the moon emerged through a break in the clouds and lit the scene with its reflected light. A man lost his grip trying to cross the rail, and fell back through the stairway doors, which gaped open like jaws to receive him. There were many such horrors that Thiger saw and wished he had not. Nonetheless, crouched safely on his perch outside of the rails, he remained cautious and composed. Since he had left the Pub Admiral, perhaps ten minutes had passed, or maybe twelve, but certainly not more. He had lost track of the acquaintance with whom he had spent the evening and escaped, and in a strange way he was in his element now, a man who knew ships, acting logically and alone, with no need to explain himself and nothing to do but survive. He rode the ship as others might ride a horse. He was steady. He was patient. Even when the list grew to 80 degrees, he kept waiting to see whether the hull would find its equilibrium and stabilize. When it did not, and he saw the funnel lie down and go under, he had the evidence he needed that the *Estonia* was inverting, and so he left the railing and began to walk down the superstructure's outsides. The ship no longer rocked much in the waves. Surf crashed over its stern, to his left. The steel underfoot was wet. He was careful not to fall through the windows into the darkened quarters below.

It is not known whether victims trapped in the cabins and common spaces saw Thiger or the others who navigated the superstructure when the hull was horizontal. From below, the escapees would have seemed like shadows in a dream, passing overhead against a pale night sky. They would have seemed like fugitives on the run. One of them put his foot through a window and was injured but not caught. There was no communication between the two worlds, which had grown impossibly far apart. In total perhaps 150 people made the trip across the outsides. By the time Thiger got to the lower hull, most of them had already arrived. A large group was bivouacked around the stabilizer fin, where it was possible to delay for a few minutes while the ship hesitated, lingering on its side. Soon, however, the movement resumed, and the group broke up as people joined the chaotic migration, chased forward and across the curvature of the bottom by the settling at the stern and the ship's continuing roll. The heel grew to 110 degrees, and later to 120 degrees and more. Some of the escapees had managed to drag life rafts with them, but they were having the standard problems getting them launched—difficulties compounded by fights that broke out and by the desperation that drove people to go piling into rafts that were still too high on the hull. Those people were difficult to dislodge, though some fell out when the rafts eventually tumbled or slid into the water. Many of the canopies did not erect. Many of the rafts flipped upside down. One riot stands for others in those apocalyptic moments: after ten people threw themselves onto an inverted raft near the aft end of the hull and others attacked en masse, trying to get on too, the entire assembly went sliding uncontrollably into the ocean upside down, with people hanging on inside and out. This was a poor way to survive the Baltic in a storm on a September night.

So was every other way, however. What difference did it make to be altruistic and brave—indeed, what difference to be grasping? These were the people who had led the race, and it was as if they had been suddenly abandoned to chance. How tame did the Baltic seem then? How subject to German engineering, to wise counsel and international regulation? Their lives had been reduced to a rolling sliver of steel, a whaleback, the outside curvature of a bilge dissolving into the sea. Between the force of the wind and the waves and the nearness of the end, there was no possibility for even the sort of embryonic society that had flickered on the Deck 7 promenade. Empty life vests and rafts, both whole and ruined, littered the water. People were scattered up and down the hull—walking, crawling, lying down—and though some seemed to cluster, each of them in practice was alone. A couple was separated when the husband jumped into the water and beckoned to his wife, and out of terror she refused to go. As one by one they were picked off by the waves, Pierre Thiger got the impression that the ocean was reaching up to fetch them and drag them down. His own turn was coming soon. The ship had rolled to 135 degrees, halfway from prone to fully inverted, and the waves were surging all around. The water was so close that when a lifeboat that had broken loose smashed against the hull, Thiger was showered by pieces of shattered fiberglass.

The wave that took him caught him by surprise, hitting so quickly that he didn't see it coming, and he had no chance to draw a breath. He was pulled below the surface, came up, and was pulled below again on what seemed to him to be a long, long trip. The ocean bubbled and roared around his ears. Then he rose, and though he seemed to be drifting upward forever, and though he swallowed water several times, he did not breathe the water in, and eventually he arrived on the surface. Empty life vests floated in abundance there, and he caught hold of several, as well as a wooden plank for good measure. Driven by the winds, a line of life rafts disappeared behind the hull, like a string of pearls, Thiger thought, or a saint's day procession. The waves seemed mountainous from his swimmer's height. They bore down on him with speed, carried him upslope to the crests, and then dropped him behind as they rushed on, hissing into the night. Many of them were breaking, throwing powerful white cascades down their forward slopes, leaving scars of foam on their trails. The air was full of spume and spray. Thiger heard a frightened swimmer nearby, calling for help. Encumbered by his vests, he paddled over to assist him as best he could—presumably by snaring additional flotation gear. When he looked back at the *Estonia*, it was showing its keel and slowly sliding below the surface on a steep angle, stern first. It had raised its bulbous bow so high that parts of the bridge remained clear. Ever the observer, Thiger was one of those who noticed that the entire front end was missing—that the ship's bow visor somehow had fallen off. There was no time to think about that now. He watched the ocean flood into the bridge. He spotted a life raft, swam to it, and got in. It was characteristic of Thiger that he did not cower in fear but sat up to look outside. He watched the ship disappear. There was no whirlpool sucking things down. The surface bubbled and boiled for a while, and then did not. The life raft was treated violently by the waves, but several hours later Thiger was winched to safety by a helicopter and delivered to a rescue ship, the *Symphony* of the Silja Line. The *Symphony* in turn delivered him to Stockholm, where he went ashore grateful to be alive, but shocked by the death of so many others.

Survival in the water was of course a desperate affair. The night was rent with the cries of invisible victims pleading for help, then growing weak with the cold, moaning, going silent, and losing the fight to stay alive. Nothing could be done for them. Those without life vests simply slipped away. Those with life vests died on the surface, alone among the waves. Many who found their way to life rafts could not get in. Many who got in were then washed out and had to get in all over again. Some did not succeed. Some did succeed, only to die once inside. The horror aboard the life rafts was compounded by anonymity and confusion. Twenty-two life rafts were occupied. They were not the protective cocoons one might imagine, but flimsy assemblies of inflated tubes, half collapsed, that were flipped repeatedly by the breaking waves, flushed with frigid water, and often indistinguishable from the pandemonium of the sea. Attempts to organize their collective history will always suffer from the incoherence of that history as it was actually lived. The JAIC later tried to sort things out using bureaucratic technique—cross-referencing the survivors' statements and assigning letters to the lifeboats in a progression from A to V. But even its official report reads like a kaleidoscope of fear.

LIFE RAFT M

One passenger crawled into a raft on the *Estonia's* hull. Other people threw themselves on top of the canopy of this raft. The raft slid and got stuck on the fender. Another passenger standing on top of the raft saw about twenty people running along the hull towards him. Several threw themselves on top of the canopy. It seemed dangerous to launch the raft from this height and they were arguing about whether the ship would stay afloat or sink. When the angle was favourable they dragged the raft towards the bridge where several rafts were floating in the water. As the raft slid, this witness was sitting and facing the direction of travel. When the raft hit the water, the witness was struck in the face by a floating object and fell overboard bleeding severely. He saw two rafts with the canopies released blowing towards him and managed to catch one of them. This raft was violently thrown by the waves several times against the hull of the *Estonia*.

The passenger who was under the canopy had to get out because the raft was full of water. He lost his trousers and shoes while fighting his way out and was completely naked.

He managed to get over to another raft with several people inside and some on top of the canopy. He had the feeling that people were being exchanged by the waves, i.e. that some were washed into the sea and others were coming on board. He heard calls for help and screaming outside and tried for a long time to pull a man into the raft, holding on to him asking for help from others inside the raft. One man could not help because he was bleeding severely and could not bend his face forward, and another was powerless to help because of an injured back. After about ten minutes he let the man go because he was afraid of losing all his remaining strength in attempting to pull him up or even holding him. Because of the water in the raft and because the waves were constantly flattening the canopy, he stood up to hold the canopy in place.

A third witness managed to grasp a rope to this life raft. He reported that there were numerous people in the water and around the raft, many in panic. People were climbing onto his back and he got several bruises and scratches. The raft was thrown against the hull several times by the heavy seas. He got squeezed between the raft and the hull several times but by bracing his feet against the hull he managed to get on the raft. During the struggle he injured his back against the hull.

Another witness reported that the raft slid down "at full speed" and that he jumped off. He fell into the water, hitting his head and his back. He swam towards this raft but found nothing to hang on to. A woman on it took his hand and held it. Several people in the water clung to his back and around his face. He also got a hand in his mouth. He got help from the woman to get onto the raft and when interviewed he stated that he could not have made it without her help.

This raft collided with another and the witness with the face injury managed to get hold of it. Several people climbed on his back to the other raft and when he lost his grip there were only five remaining, four male passengers and one woman, all Swedish.

The witness with the face injury has reported that one man was very active. He tried for over an hour to pull aboard a younger Estonian man but did not have the strength and the man eventually disappeared after calling for help in Estonian for quite a while. This witness also reported that there was a great deal of water in the raft and one male passenger stood naked, holding the canopy for most of the time. This witness could not move, let alone help because every movement increased the bleeding. (Later at the hospital, this man was found to have five facial fractures.)

The witness who held up the canopy has reported that an injured man in the raft was bleeding heavily from the face and holding the head of a woman above the water. The woman was wearing a brassiere and panties only. Occasionally waves flattened the canopy, causing this witness to fall. Every time, he forced it up again. While standing, he tried to close the openings to prevent any more water from coming in. He found the ropes to control the openings but did not find any place to fasten them and he therefore held them tight. He was standing for about four hours and became very tired.

The others tried to fire distress rockets but one of them ignited inside the raft, filling it with smoke. No one was able to throw the rocket out and this witness had to stick his head outside for air. The woman, he reported, was becoming more and more listless and limp. She occasionally slid down into the water in the raft and was pulled up by others, who tried to massage her and shake her to arouse her. One hour prior to their rescue she died.

After several hours the sea movement changed. Water entered the raft and pushed down the canopy again. The occupants found nothing to bail with and have said that by now it was only a matter of minutes before they would have to give up. They were not able to struggle anymore in a raft filled with water and with the canopy down.

They were saved by a Finnish helicopter at dawn . . .

This is what awaits you after you rush up the stairs and succeed in escaping from a sinking Baltic ferry. The rafts were like mountain tents sheltering desperate climbers caught out in a killer storm—thin-walled and impossibly precarious, but absolutely vital. Each contained a tiny world of misery. Afterward, the occupants' memories were by definition narrow and incomplete. They were images of huddled strangers trying to endure an unendurable night.

LIFE RAFT C

She thought she was going to die so she inhaled water. She eventually rose to the surface where she could see the *Estonia* and people clinging on. She collected several life-jackets from around her and floated on them towards a raft. She had difficulties getting on it and a young man from inside reached out to her. It took some time because she had tied herself to ropes, but the young man, an Estonian, held

on and eventually pulled her up. In this raft there were six
people some of whom were wearing overalls with "Estline"
printed on them. Together they managed to release the
canopy and got lights in the raft. From the water they
heard screaming but were not able to see anyone.

LIFE RAFT I

Cascades of water entered the raft at every wave and it was
already full of water. A few bailed and they managed to
close the opening after about 45 minutes. They could hear
people in the water calling for help but were unable to see
from where because of the darkness and the big waves.
Many of them could do nothing to help because they were
too exhausted. A few struggled with a crew member over a
hand torch. The crew member held desperately on to the
torch. They eventually managed to loosen his grip and start
signaling with it. The people in the raft tried to lie very
close together to keep warm but they were moved around
by the water inside and the heavy sea. At dawn the responding ferry *Isabella* came upon the raft, and lowered
one of its own, attached to wires, along with three crewmen dressed in survival suits, to help handle the transfer.
The *Estonia's* raft struck the *Isabella's* hull repeatedly but
after a while one survivor after another started to haul
themselves over to the *Isabella's* raft, which by this time
was filling with water. *Isabella* crew members made several
attempts to hoist the raft and the crew members in survival
suits eventually jumped into the water so as to lessen the
weight. After about ten attempts they managed to lift the
raft, but the bottom split and all but one of those on board

fell into the sea . . . Several came under the raft and some disappeared in the water.

LIFE RAFT K

The Swedish passenger managed to climb onto a life raft which was floating upside down. On board were two girls in their twenties. The Estonian repairman swam for about ten minutes before being hauled on board by the others. All four of them lay close together to keep warm and also massaged and hugged each other. Waves sprayed over them constantly, and washed them into the water four or five times. Each time they helped each other back on board, someone always managing to hold on to some part of the raft. The men wanted to turn the raft the right way up but the girls were very nervous and afraid of going into the water voluntarily to make this possible. When a wave once again washed over the raft, the two girls slid away and disappeared. The last thing the witnesses heard was one of them groaning.

LIFE RAFT O

One Swedish passenger jumped into the sea and came up close to a raft floating upside down. He got a grip and managed to hold on for a while. Suddenly a wave turned the raft right-side-up and the next wave washed this person into it. There was much water inside and he was alone. After about fifteen minutes he heard calls for help but was unable to see anyone in the darkness. Some time later a wave overturned the raft again and then immediately another one righted it. After this he realized that there was another man in the raft, an Estonian crew member.

LIFE RAFT S

One Estonian passenger in the water saw a raft after a while, but was unable to reach it. After another twenty minutes in the sea he was dragged on board this raft by other people. It was full of water and people were lying together with their arms around one another to keep warm. The water made them slide around in the raft and it was difficult to stay on board without holding on to a rope or something else. One witness remembered that several people disappeared during the night. Several others were washed overboard several times but managed to get a grip on something and pull themselves aboard again. At times there was panic in the raft and several people died. One witness said there were six or seven dead by the morning. During the rescue by helicopter one person fell back into the sea and was killed.

LIFE RAFT T

He could not see where he was but later found he was under a life raft which was floating upside down. The canopy was released, and he managed to sit and stand inside this. On top of the upside-down raft there were three other men and he managed to contact them by pounding on the bottom of the raft above him. One of the men on top of the raft, the trainee second officer, had been clinging on for a while unable to get onto it because his feet were caught in ropes. His lifejacket had slid down and was hanging around his waist. A boy helped him up. Lying on top of this upside-down raft there was also a naked elderly man. The passenger under the raft shouted to the others on top not to forget him. After several hours he heard a helicopter and he pounded on the bottom again with the help of a distress rocket, afraid he would be forgotten. When the helicopter rescue man had hoisted the men off the top of the raft, he and the Swede below it were able to localize each other by pounding on the raft. The rescue man made a slit in the bottom with his knife and the passenger dragged himself out through this.

LIFE RAFT U

One person took the lead. Several were without lifejackets, some quite passive, one rather drunk and wearing only underpants. He got upset and started to fight with the leader, who tried to calm him down and to protect himself. The man fought violently and was not easily calmed. After about an hour, this man died in the arms of another passenger. Somewhat later another man started to fight with the leader, and there was some tumult but this man calmed down after a while. He was hanging on to a rope in the middle of the raft. He had suddenly become violent, shouting in English about knives, evidently wanting to cut his way out through the canopy. Two men died during the night, one with a heart disease and the drunk man already mentioned ... After about two hours, witnesses heard someone outside the raft and managed to pull aboard a German passenger who had been swimming all the time. This person smelled strongly of diesel oil.

Rolf Sörman never found even such late shelter in a raft. When he took Yvonne Bernevall's hand and dropped with her from Deck 8 into the frigid sea, he knew that he was going to die. He gave himself a few minutes at the most until he would succumb to the cold. When he did survive—and was ultimately airlifted to safety—he credited his life to the adrenaline load that had coursed through his veins. Physiologists might disagree, but there is no question that his body's instinctive defenses played a primary role. He was so wired that the water did not feel cold to him when he plunged in.

When he hit the water, Sörman kept holding Bernevall's hand. They went deep, and Sörman cleared his ears twice before the life vests prevailed over the momentum of their fall and they started floating upward. Near the top, Sörman was hit in the head by the foot of a frantic swimmer, and he yanked his hand from Bernevall's grasp in order to protect himself. For some seconds after he surfaced, he thought she might have drowned, but then she appeared nearby. He swam over to her, and they clung together for a moment to keep from being driven apart by the force of the waves. They talked. They had a sense of being tugged from below, as if they were in the clutches of a vertical drift caused by the hull's subsidence. Staying closely together, they swam away for about twenty-five yards against the oncoming seas until the sensation diminished. Again they held each other and talked. It was essential that they find something to float on. Their position upwind from the *Estonia* gave them no chance of reaching the life rafts, which could not be secured or delayed on this, the storm-bashed upweather side of the ship, and which, once released, went scooting downwind to the east. The situation was not entirely hopeless, however, because the *Estonia* itself was drifting eastward, slowing as it sank but continuing to litter the waves in its trail with waterlogged, wind-resistant debris. Sörman and Bernevall struggled through the flotsam, hoping to discover an object large enough to serve as a raft—furniture, for instance, or a section of wooden planking. It later turned out that one survivor did ride a wooden cupboard for a while, but Sörman and Bernevall were not so lucky. They found nothing of use, and instead came suddenly upon a scene of the dead and dying, a cluster of corpses lying face-down in the waves, and among them several people still alive but thrashing violently during the final throes of drowning. In their haste to avoid entanglement, Sörman and Bernevall split apart— he striking to the left, she to the right. Minutes later, when they tried to join up again, they could not. Sörman saw her floating high on top of a wave when he was at its bottom. He swam for her, but when he saw her next, she had drifted farther away. After that she was lost.

Sörman turned to swim back toward the *Estonia* when suddenly his life vest came off, the flotation collar peeling over his head. He jammed it back on and tightened the straps, but it came off again. Five times this happened in rapid succession, reducing Sörman to near panic, until he realized that the wind from behind was to blame. He turned his back again on the *Estonia*, which solved the problem. He then tried to build a raft by stacking up ten squares of the rubberized deck matting that he found nearby. The squares were not designed to float, and they barely did, offering little more support in combination than alone. Sörman had to give up on his raft. At that point, however, an overturned lifeboat came into view, riding bow-down and low, with its keel just a few inches above the surface. The front end was completely smashed in. Sörman had the impression that the lifeboat had just emerged from the depths. He swam to it and squirmed up onto the keel, emerging partially from the water. As many as seven others did the same, including the heroic third engineer. The weakest was a young woman dancer who had a nasty head wound and was very frightened. Sörman grabbed her by her jacket and began his second losing fight for the life of a woman that night.

Conditions on the overturned lifeboat were extraordinarily tough, with wind-driven rain and ocean spray as cold as sleet, as well as breaking waves that kept sweeping across the hull. The man who had found the safest position, at the stern, made no attempt to help the others, and he clung with both hands to the propeller shaft in a full-blown panic, wailing prayers and loudly calling to God. For the sake of his own nerves and the courage of others, Sörman shouted at him repeatedly to stop, but the man was beyond reach, and he did not. The overturned lifeboat drifted directly toward the mutilated front end of the *Estonia's* hull, now heavily inverted and in the last stages of sinking into the sea. Aboard the lifeboat, nothing could be done but to go for the ride. At the last moment, just when it seemed they might be smashed against the hull, they were swept slightly forward and began to pass directly under the bulbous bow. An instant later, in the confusion of a nightmare, they passed into the flooded entrance of a huge dark tunnel that was swallowing the surging waves. It was the open end of the car deck, the ship's voracious mouth. Sörman realized that he had not escaped the *Estonia* after all, that it would catch him now and take him down. Unable to endure the sight, he turned his head away in fear. When finally he found the courage to look again, the *Estonia* was gone.

The sinking of the *Estonia* was by no means the most lethal shipping accident in recent times. That distinction belongs to a Japanese-built passenger vessel named the *Doña Paz*, which had been wrecked once already and rebuilt, and was sailing as an interisland ferry in the Philippines when on the night of December 20, 1987, in good weather, it collided with a small tanker carrying 8,800 barrels of petroleum products. A ferocious fire engulfed both ships, incinerating all but two of the tanker's crew of thirteen. On the *Doña Paz*, the slaughter was horrendous. All 58 of the crew perished, and only 21 passengers escaped alive. The ship had been licensed to carry 1,518 passengers and, according to its official manifest, had squeezed 1,586 aboard. In reality, it turned out to have been overloaded by a factor of nearly three. By final approximation, 4,375 people died. Roughly a thousand of them were children, traveling on Christmas holiday. Because crew error was to blame (and the crews were dead), the companies were not held responsible. The accident was not quite considered to be business as usual—there was more than normal frustration expressed in the Manila papers—but the truth is that ferry accidents have occurred regularly in the Philippines for a long time, and probably always will. This is equally true in nearby Indonesia. It is not that the deaths are easier to endure there, as it may seem from a distance, but that the context of poverty and corruption overwhelms them. Accidents of whatever kind are part of the confusion involved in the larger struggle for life. And when a ferry goes down, it is almost guaranteed to be overcrowded—a matter as much of economic necessity as opportunism and exploitation.

Indeed, in most cases of Third World ferry accidents, the overcrowding itself is what triggers the loss. On the evening of May 20, 1996, for instance, a 195-foot Tanzanian ferry named the *Bukoba* left its home port of the same name on Lake Victoria for a regular overnight run, carrying a heavy cargo of bananas and (apparently) the maximum permissible load of 441 ticket-bearing passengers.

At its first stop, about fifteen miles down the coast, more bananas were piled on the deck, and hundreds of passengers—who had been unable to board at Bukoba and had chased after the ship by truck—rushed up the gangplank in typical riotous style (some no doubt falling into the water). When the *Bukoba* set off again, it was listing to starboard. It was a seventeen-year-old Belgian-built vessel, owned and operated by the same Tanzanian Railways Corporation that runs the Meyer Werft–built *Liemba*, of *African Queen* fame. Seven years earlier, in 1989, the *Bukoba* had been deemed dangerously top-heavy by a team of visiting Belgian engineers who had recommended that modifications be carried out. Such work was never performed. Now, in the early morning hours, having rolled strangely all night despite calm seas, the *Bukoba* made a turn and suddenly listed sharply to starboard. The crew shouted at the passengers to move to the other side, and they stampeded, causing the ship to capsize, after which it immediately rolled upside down. Between 600 and 1,000 people drowned. Many were trapped in air pockets for hours, until a rescue crew cut holes in the hull and unintentionally let the air out, sending the ship to the bottom. One of the victims is said to have been a former Egyptian police officer named Ubaida Al-Banshiri, who was the cofounder of al Qaeda and at the time of his death was its military commander. Among the more bizarre claims now made about Osama Bin Laden is that he subsequently "investigated" the accident. If so, he learned nothing that wasn't obvious from the start. People weigh a lot, and when frightened, they tend to flock. You can't just load them onto a ship without concern for the balance.

This is a lesson repeated without end. A more recent example occurred on the night of September 26, 2002, when a Senegalese ferry named the *Joola* capsized in a squall off the Gambian coast while making the trip from the troubled southern province of Casamance north to the capital city, Dakar. The *Joola* was licensed for 536 passengers but carried at least twice that many. When wind and violent rain suddenly drove the passengers en masse to one side of the ship, the *Joola* rolled over, and a thousand people died. Senegal, one of the proudest African states, responded by unseating two government ministers and mounting an official investigation. There were a few testimonies of the sort that emerged from the *Estonia*, but there really wasn't much to conclude. The loading had been a typically West African affair—less harsh than ferry loadings in say Haiti or Bangladesh, but chaotic nonetheless. The ship sailed only once a week from Casamance, providing a welcome alternative to the difficult overland journey to the capital, which included the risk of rebel attack and an expensive river crossing. Many of the travelers were market women burdened heavily with their bundles of goods. The crew allowed them all to board, as much in solidarity with them as for the small additional income that could be gleaned.

Afterward, the Senegalese government blamed the captain for not performing formal stability calculations, as if the paperwork could have kept the poverty of Casamance away. It pretended that the capsize was a nautical incident and that the investigation might lead to meaningful technical reforms. Outsiders had a more skeptical view and tended to treat the capsize (if they noticed it at all) as just another Third World ferry disaster—the inevitable extension of hopelessly chaotic shores. It merited at most the front page in a few French newspapers for part of a week, and then it faded rapidly from view. In the summer of 2003 a similar slaughter in Bangladesh merited barely page 2. A few months later, in the fall of 2003, another big loss on the river Congo was virtually indistinguishable from the region's civil wars. There is no doubt that racism played a role in the lack of response, but it was also simply the track record of these nations that caused the world to turn away. Their cities were impossibly overloaded. Was there any reason to expect that their ships wouldn't be?

The same logic run in reverse drove the strong reactions to the *Estonia's* loss. With few exceptions, the victims had been middle-class, pale-skinned Nordics, who in the consciousness of the world's most powerful publics were a close and familiar type. More important, the ship had been sailing between northern European shores, to Sweden of all places, a country so reasonable and sedate that it hadn't fought a war in two hundred years and was totally unprepared for this outbreak of anarchy. Estonia too was unprepared. It had suffered the successive traumas of alternating German and Russian occupations, and as an independent state, it was somewhat unformed—young, insecure, a bit prone to criminality—but even so, compared with Africa or South Asia it was a regular little Switzerland of law and procedure, a *bürgerlich* nation. On the half-empty boulevards of Tallinn, pedestrians waited for the lights to flash WALK even when no cars were in sight. There was a black market, just as there was smuggling in the harbor, but even that was in a sense just evidence of regulation. For the passengers politely filing onto the *Estonia* on September 27, there was not the slightest risk of falling off the gangplanks, and no reason to suspect that this well-painted ship might kill them. Its papers were in order. Its crews were certified. That same day, it had passed the very model of a port state inspection. Estonians had done the work, but under the watchful eyes of Swedish mentors. Other Swedish mentors were aboard, scattered among the crew. Those mentors were the advisers employed by the ship's

Swedish co-owner, Nordström & Thulin, which also had formal responsibility for the ship's technical management. The involvement of front companies in Cyprus and Luxembourg was just another sign of the sophistication and modernity of the setup. Estonia was now a part of the modern world. The ship may have been slightly out of balance when it sailed, but it was far from overloaded. According to the highest standards of international regulation, it was guaranteed to be safe. Its loss was a shock because it was an aberration.

That was all the more reason for a thorough inquiry. The JAIC succeeded only partially; having set off in the right direction, it stopped short of going all the way. It was not the cabal it was said to be, but rather a fractious multinational group steered by officials who had little working knowledge of the sea, whose careers had led them to think in terms primarily of written regulation, and who had risen high enough within their respective governments to have become naturally sensitive to diplomacy and the concerns of bureaucratic constituencies. Surrounded as they were by crowds of outsiders—survivors, witnesses, and theorists, all clamoring for attention—they made the serious mistake of ignoring public relations, and they closed in on themselves without holding public forums or even pretending to listen to disparate views. As a result, they developed an unnecessary reputation for secretiveness that nourished the conspiracy theorists and eventually undermined their own good work. They made technical mistakes too. The most blatant was their strange and categorical claim that when the *Estonia* sailed from Tallinn on the night of its demise, nearly everything was right with its maintenance and equipment, and that in the important matters, its condition was almost as good as new. One needed to know none of the details to suspect that this could not have been true. Nothing is ever completely right aboard a ship. Of course it is possible that the JAIC actually believed what it said. It is possible that it was so invested in shore-bound administrative views that it accepted the *Estonia's* documentation at face value and bought in to the assurances by the ship's managers, crew, and advisers that everything aboard was always done by the book. Nonetheless, the idea that a fourteen-year-old ferry in the hands of a Soviet-trained crew could have been in nearly perfect condition seemed to defy the nature of the world.

Rolf Sörman, who now works as the assistant headmaster of a secondary school in Stockholm, recently explained the JAIC's stance to me in regional political terms. He did not see the need to invent conspiracies. He said that after the birth of the Estonian state in 1991, Swedish maritime officials had received instructions to help this new and welcomed neighbor to establish a ferry line— assistance that involved active participation with the authorities in Tallinn, and which, although it did not require laws or regulations to be broken, invited a certain relaxation of controls. The Swedish bureaucracy, in other words, felt implicated in the accident, as did the Finnish one, for similar reasons. Both were well represented on the JAIC, which after its formation just naturally took a defensive position, as bureaucracies do. Sörman said, "All authorities lie sometimes. And if you've started to lie, you can't stop. You can't go backward and say you were wrong." I asked him whether perhaps the bind was worse in Scandinavia because of the moralistic traditions there. He grew prickly, and took a jab at the United States. He was nobody's fool.

Neither was Meyer Werft's attorney, Peter Holtappels. Recognizing the vulnerabilities of the JAIC in this regard—the first step toward laying the blame on the ship's design—he had the experts in his German Group bear down on the question of the *Estonia*'s condition at the time of its final departure. They had the advantage of not having to abide by the sort of rules that would have applied in a court of law. They also had plenty of time, money, and personnel. Not surprisingly, they found a lot that was wrong. By working around the edges of the statements that had been made about the afternoon's port state inspection, they assembled enough circumstantial evidence to make a tenuous but plausible case that the inspection had gone less smoothly than the JAIC had been led to believe. According to this alternative version, the visiting Swedish inspectors had been so worried by what they were seeing that they had tried to have the *Estonia* detained—a radical action that, according to the German Group, the Estonians had refused to take. An attempt to go beyond them, to the Swedish maritime authorities back in Stockholm, had resulted in stern orders from Sweden to remain silent and acquiesce. The simplicity and timing of this little drama, with Estonians playing the villains just hours before the accident, seems too well tailored to be real, and it has repeatedly been denied by the inspectors involved. Still it raises doubts, if for no other reason than the equally simplistic counterclaims by those same inspectors that, according to the JAIC, "the vessel was in good condition and very well maintained."

The focus was on the bow. Holtappels and the JAIC agreed that the rubber seals around the bow visor had gone bad, allowing water to leak freely into the bow cavity when the ship was under way. This was the caveat in the JAIC's otherwise positive assessment of the ship's condition, a problem that the inspectors had reported and that the Finns subsequently found affecting as many as half of the ferries in their fleets. Judging from the stains on the inside of the *Estonia's* visor, the water typically stood several feet high, at about the same height as the bow wake and just above the level of the car deck. The JAIC reasoned that the leakage, though undesirable, had not affected the seaworthiness of the ship, largely because the bow ramp in its proper up-and-locked position would have kept anything beyond a trickle from flowing onto the car deck. The JAIC report added that the water's proportionately small weight did not appreciably affect the critical upward loads on the bow, and concluded that the leaks around the visor were irrelevant to the *Estonia's* demise.

Holtappels strongly disagreed, and he was willing to go where the JAIC was not, beyond the cautious testimonies of the crew and inspectors, and out among the crowds of ordinary witnesses, mostly passengers, who had nothing to fear from saying the wrong thing and who, having been ignored by the authorities, were all the more eager to talk. Meyer Werft had a field day with them that extended for years. It turned out that many of the passengers who might have appeared to the crew to be mere landlubbers while aboard—a little dumb as they sat in the bars or browsed through the duty-free shops—were in fact acute and credible observers of maritime technicalities. Some were also frequent travelers on this run, or they had survived the final trip, or had professional knowledge of the sea, or some combination of the above. In any case, Holtappels had plenty of testimonies to choose from, and when he needed more, he flew people to Hamburg, to his law office. He was not a man to take partial measures. In the end he built a powerful and convincing case that the bow visor was not only leaking but badly misaligned, and furthermore that the bow ramp had been so severely twisted that for months it could not be fully closed and sealed. In the final analysis, this meant that even in normal weather, salt water could not be kept off the car deck and routinely had to be drained away through the scuppers.

Holtappels's star witness in the matter was a Turkish-born entrepreneur, age forty-two at the time of the accident, who had emigrated to Sweden in 1980 and, upon taking citizenship, had changed his name from Kadir Kaymaz to Carl Övberg. He worked as a truck driver, but for several years now he had been engaged in a sideline, buying used Volvos in Sweden and taking them by ferry to Tallinn, where he sold them. As a result, he had ridden the *Estonia* forty times, and he had been aboard the ship in the economy section on Deck 1 on the night it went down. Three years later, having been interviewed for German TV by the crusading Jutta Rabe (presumably because the ship's hostesses had appeared "nervous" to him upon departure from Tallinn), he summarized his technical observations for Holtappels's agents in Stockholm with a statement in good English that runs to eight single-spaced pages and is supplemented by photographs of the bow ramp (with explanatory arrows), deck plans, a hand-drawn sketch of his escape up a lower stairway, and, for good measure, a map of the Baltic.

Övberg was a remarkably observant man. He said, for instance, "It was clearly visible that the bow ramp was severely misaligned, respectively bent. In open condition the port side was much lower compared to the starboard side. The bow ramp could not be opened in one go, but had to be raised/lowered several times before it was finally down." He could provide plenty of detail, too. He reported that the bow ramp was so twisted that when it was lowered to the dock it rested on the port side only, and required the crew to place rope coils under the starboard side to support the weight of the vehicles rolling on or off the ship. He said, "I am also of the opinion that, at least during the last months before the catastrophe, the bow ramp could not be closed completely anymore, because several times I observed from my position at the fore part of the car deck that light was falling onto the car deck as soon as the (outer) visor began to open, i.e. before the bow ramp itself was even moved. This, in my opinion, is only possible if the bow ramp was already open to a certain extent when the visor opened. The light came in as shown on the photo on Enclosure No. 5 at the upper port side."

Holtappels must have been thrilled. Here was his passenger from heaven, an innocent victim with a strong memory and a good eye for bad behavior—an unimpeachable *Estonia* spotter. True, his style was sometimes a little strained ("The area with missing flaps at the port side of the closed bow ramp can be seen on picture 1 of Enclosure No. 1, where it is indicated by arrow 1."), and he may have required some coaching, but by 1997, on point after point, he was delivering just the sort of backup Holtappels needed. Övberg had seen the *Estonia* used brutally as an icebreaker in the winter, smashing hard against the floes to make its way. He gave examples of the crew's typically crude "Eastern Bloc" attitudes toward safety. He said that despite announcements to the contrary, the car-deck doors remained unlocked when the ship was at sea, and that he often visited his vehicles to check on their safety. Once, on an ordinary passage to Tallinn in calm weather, he had found the car deck covered with two inches of water, apparently because the scuppers couldn't drain fast enough to keep up with the flow. It is not clear whether he realized at the time that this was unsafe, though certainly the crew must have. Övberg said he commonly saw the deckhands struggling up front with their heavy tools, torching and sledgehammering the bow ramp, or cycling the hydraulic pumps to make the ramp behave—and not only at dockside but while the ship was under way. On the night of the ship's demise, he heard similar noises again—sledgehammer blows, though from somewhere aft of the bow, and hydraulics under load. These noises led after a while to the large crashes, and the first heavy heel.

There were many other testimonies, none quite so complete, but several attesting to incidents of water on the car deck during the year preceding the accident. Presumably the water was not there on every trip, perhaps because the crew had grown adept at improvised solutions, including plugging the gaps along the bow ramp's port side with rags and mattresses. The problem was that these solutions sometimes failed. The most alarming evidence of this arrived in the form of a letter from a mariner who, by profession, was expected to be a placid, reliable sort of man—a Swedish-waters pilot, now retired, named Bo Soderman, who the previous Christmas, nine months before the accident, had twice guided the *Estonia* inbound through the Swedish archipelago. His letter seems to have been addressed to one of Holtappels's agents, and in context it is endearingly sincere. It finishes by saying, "In case I can contribute to solve the *Estonia* question in a seamanlike way, I am willing to cooperate." It starts with an experience in December 1993, when he boarded the ship in moderate seas, and to his surprise found the entire starboard side of the car deck covered with several inches of water. Several days later, he prepared to board the ship again, this time in heavier seas. He wrote, "Upon my recommendation the master turned to starboard to make leeway for the pilot boat. I jumped on board from the upper platform of the pilot boat. The *Estonia*'s port pilot door was open. Under such conditions one has to expect water splashing up from below between ferry and pilot boat. This time, however, surprisingly the water came from above out of the pilot door when the *Estonia* rolled to port. When I came on board the mate warned me that there was 'plenty of water on deck!'" Indeed there was. On the way to the elevator in the center casing, he had to wade through water that came nearly to the top of his boots, and he observed waves sloshing about three feet high against the bulkheads. He wrote that he did not know where the water came from.

But Holtappels knew, and when he wrote his sea story, it went roughly as follows: Objectively speaking, Meyer Werft is an excellent shipyard, and it has endured for more than two hundred years in an increasingly competitive market, not by cutting corners, but by insisting on the old-world principles of fine workmanship and honest dealings. (Indeed, if you happen to be in the market for a new passenger ship, or would like to convert your freighter to a livestock carrier—for sheep, cattle, horses, camels—you might give Meyer Werft a call.) The *Estonia* had originally reflected that quality. It had once been a strong and confident ship, and in Finnish hands, under its former names, it had been expertly sailed and well maintained. But then at age eleven it had been sold, and in the Tallinn–Stockholm trade it had fallen rapidly into disrepair, largely because of harsh treatment and neglect by the new Estonian managers and crews. The Swedish co-owners at Nordström & Thulin were to blame too, since they were formally in charge of maintenance, but despite putting advisers aboard, in practice they were willing mostly just to go along for the ride. The JAIC had denied that the arrangement constituted a "flag of convenience" operation, but for these Swedish business interests it very much did. They would take their profits where they could, pay the insurance, and leave their Estonian partners at the helm. These Estonians were not the *bürgerlich* types that their certificates showed them to be. They were jaywalkers in traffic, smokers at the pump, ocean outlaws of the recalcitrant Soviet style. On the bridge, they crammed the ship's documents onto shelves so haphazardly that they couldn't find them again (a habit especially upsetting to Germans). They submitted to inspections, but performed minimal repairs. They seemed to care about paint. They seemed to care about schedule. But once offshore they ignored even common-sense standards of seamanship and safety. Their recklessness was known to Scandinavian officials but overlooked, because danger, like safety, is never absolute. And it was just as Rolf Sörman said: the pressure was on to encourage this new nation and to treat it with respect. The Scandinavians therefore got tangled in its web.

Holtappels wrote that when the *Estonia* sailed from Tallinn on the final evening, it was grossly unprepared for the weather ahead. Its bow visor was leaking as usual, and it was improperly latched. The bow ramp was even worse, having been partially secured only by means of an improvised arrangement of ropes and cables. The gap on its port side was stuffed with rags, blankets, and mattresses. The visor filled with seawater to the level of the bow wave, and as the ship accelerated to its full speed, that water began to spill onto the car deck. The crew was accustomed to this. The water entered as usual through the gaps at the bottom of the ramp along the port side, and because of the ship's slight list and tail-down trim, it flowed aft and starboard across the deck floor. Presumably the scuppers drained it away adequately at first, but within an hour or two, as the *Estonia* rushed onward into the growing waves, the level of the water inside the visor rose, and the flow onto the car deck increased until the scuppers could no longer keep up. The crew responded with typical improvisational bravado by cracking open the starboard loading ramp at the stern (think "tailgate") to allow the excess water to drain overboard into the ship's wake. The car deck in other words was turned into a channel, with water cascading in at one end, rippling among the tires of the parked vehicles, and exiting at the other. The configuration was probably sustainable if the weather grew no worse, but it was highly unorthodox nonetheless, particularly for a ship proceeding into a heavy storm.

There is some evidence that this sequence of events did in fact occur. Rolf Sörman at the time was trying to hold his seminar in an aft conference room, and he had to call off the meeting because of the sustained whine of a hydraulic pump on the car deck immediately below—a pump that would have been run to keep the stern ramp cracked open. Moreover, the ramp was in that position when the wreck was finally surveyed. The JAIC believed that the ramp had been knocked open when the stern of the inverted ferry hit the sea floor and pivoted on that corner. But if Holtappels is right and the crew opened the ramp to counter massive early flooding, it means that Silver Linde and the other surviving sailors subsequently lied when they testified (or implied) that the car deck was dry until nearly the end. Such lies would hardly be surprising. The JAIC itself acknowledged that much of Silver Linde's testimony seemed contradictory. More difficult to understand, however, was the attitude of the trainee officer Einar Kukk, who left the bridge after midnight, and—at the height of the storm on his first trip aboard, presumably with a torrent now flowing through the ship—felt relaxed enough to stop casually by the Pub Admiral (where he saw Linde) before heading to his cabin and undressing. Kukk was a Soviet-trained sailor, true, but would he have had so little concern for his own survival?

It was around such questions that Holtappels's story began to falter. Until this point in the final voyage, the narrative in summary seemed credible enough: the *Estonia* was poorly maintained and recklessly sailed, and it had long-standing problems with the bow, well-known to the crew, which caused water to start leaking onto the car deck soon after the departure from Tallinn. Holtappels's problem was that though these revelations helped to spread the blame, they did not absolve the *Estonia*'s builders. Indeed, Meyer Werft might still have gone down to defeat had Holtappels's experts concluded, for instance, that even large leaks were unimportant, and that the cause of the accident was a bow visor failure much like the one the JAIC described—a sudden loss in heavy waves that dragged the bow ramp open because of the lack of genuine redundancy in an egregiously unsafe design. Naturally there was little worry that the experts would conclude any such thing. But Holtappels was in a writer's bind. Having revealed the *Estonia*'s dramatic predicament in the hours before midnight—he had portrayed it sailing into heavy weather with a jury-rigged bow, a growing leak, and a callous and complicit crew—he had to find a way to see the self-destruction through. Apparently this was difficult to achieve. But he was ambitious as usual. He drove the *Estonia* at full speed past the witness on the bridge of the crossing *Amber*, turned it at the waypoint on schedule in the first minutes of the new day, and then launched into a series of intricate maneuvers—of the ship, its bow components, and various members of the now-dead crew.

In places the narrative was good. Highlights included one group of sailors working frantically on the foredeck as the ship crashed through heavy waves, and another group, a secret damage-control party, finding its way to the front of the inundated car deck and operating the hydraulic pumps there in a last-ditch effort to keep the ramp at least partially closed. At the core of this

story was a classic reversal: it was not the much-maligned bow visor that had failed, Holtappels wrote, but rather the unsecured
and jury-rigged bow ramp. As the hydraulic pressure faded, the
ramp began to fall open, until, quite wonderfully, it was stopped
by the inside of the bow visor, against which it then rested, still
mostly closed. In other words, far from causing the accident, the
bow visor had nobly prolonged the *Estonia*'s life. And it kept doing it. Despite being heavy with water and improperly latched, it
held on heroically for another fifteen or twenty minutes, far into
the capsize, until it could endure the abuse no longer. At last it fell
free and glided away through the depths, coming to rest on the
seabed one mile to the west.

This was the aesthetic climax of Holtappels's story, a well-
performed flip by a trained legal mind, but it was weakened by a
practical doubt that had lingered all along, which Holtappels could
never overcome. It is obvious that flooding on the car deck as serious as that which Holtappels described would have been known to
sailors on the bridge, and very much on their mind. What kind of
crew, what kind of advisers, and particularly what kind of captain
would have kept pushing the *Estonia* at full power for hours against
the storm, past the *Amber* and through the turn, knowing that the
flooding was getting worse and that an improvised bow arrangement was coming apart? Holtappels tried taking some shots at
the dead Captain Andresson, repeating rumors that he mixed
up "port" and "starboard" and was an arrogant and incompetent
mariner. But this was weak stuff. To drive a ship to destruction
piecemeal, as Holtappels had described it, a captain would have to
be not merely arrogant and incompetent, but moronic or insane.

Holtappels must have understood the weakness of his story
line, but he was an operator, not an aspiring novelist. His work had

cost Meyer Werft—what, millions of dollars? He would not tell. In Hamburg in May 2000, after all the years he had spent on this inquiry, after all the digging that he and his team had done, he concluded the entire voluminous document with four sentences bringing up a completely different scenario—the possibility after all that the ship had been sunk by a bomb. Then he signed his name.

On the surface this was strange. It was as if the several thousand pages preceding didn't really count, as if he wasn't convinced by his story after all. But Holtappels as usual was ahead of the game. He had done his job so well that many of the victims' families now sympathized with Meyer Werft and thought of Holtappels as their friend. In return he had written them a little dedication on the first page: "To those who lost their lives, those who are still missing, their relatives and the survivors." It was a daring move, but he had mastered the terrain. When pressed, he admitted that his work had been dedicated in reality rather strictly to his clients. But with the briefest mention of illicit dives, doctored videos, explosions at the bow, and persistent "reports" of a big hole on the wreck's inaccessible starboard side, he could maintain the pressure on the Scandinavian governments at no additional effort or expense. The conspiracists had been waiting to see what he could give them. While waving good-bye from his office windows, Holtappels had leaned out and tossed them a bone.

———

By perverse laws of human nature, after the JAIC disbanded, in 1997, the best of its former members stood nearly alone, continuing for years to absorb the accusations and attacks. The most knowledgeable of them—and therefore in a sense the most lonely—was a Finnish naval architect named Tuomo Karppinen, a Ph.D. specialized in seaworthiness and stability, who worked at the time as a senior scientist at a research institute and today heads Finland's small Accident Investigation Board. Predictably, Karppinen had been singled out by Holtappels's group and had come in for special abuse by Jutta Rabe. On the opening page of the glossy promotional brochure for her new film she quoted him overliterally and out of context as saying, "We have at least a little bit investigated the sinking of the *Estonia*," making him seem like a weakling and a fool. In Potsdam on the eve of the film's release, she described him to me with Teutonic scorn. "The guy is a joke! A civil servant who is sorting his pens on the table!" But when I went to see him in Helsinki, I found the opposite to be true.

We met in his simple office in an outlying district of the city, on the third floor of a drab building within sight of the port. A tattered life ring from the *Estonia* hung in the hall. Karppinen turned out to be a tall, trim, considerate man, just beginning to gray, with a voice that was gentle but sure. Jutta Rabe had described her own path to see him as a "red thread" she had walked along. She had said, "There was something so major wrong. The members of the commission said, yes, we are open. We are coming from a *so* democratic country, you can ask any question you want. But whenever I came to the real questions, then they blocked." But Karppinen did not block me. We talked for hours, past closing time and into the night. He was thoughtful, technically expert, and utterly sincere. It was clear that he had been through a lot. At one point he took books down from the shelves to show me the lies that had been printed about him, and he turned directly to the pages. The attacks were so fresh that new ones could be expected. Karppinen may privately have regretted having ever gotten involved, I couldn't tell, but he was a man of conviction, and having taken on the task, he had discovered problems with the *Estonia's* design from which he could not back down. He did not dress up the JAIC. He spoke openly about the political and intellectual forces that had divided the investigation, the difficulties with the Estonian members, and the need as always for extrapolation and compromise. He said he would have taken the inquiries further had he been in charge. But he refused to acknowledge that the JAIC had glossed over the ship's condition, as I believed, and not because he was cowed or prevaricating, but because he fundamentally disagreed.

Anyway it was almost academic. He was a practical man, a sailor himself, and he had seen the evidence that mattered. However badly the ship had leaked, and however badly it had been handled, the bow had failed, the ship had capsized, and at least 852 people had died because of identifiable problems with the construction and design. It was important to face those facts, Karppinen believed—not to engage in moralizing or to assign blame, but to provide engineers and their regulators with the sort of real information that would allow them to write new standards and reduce the chance of such accidents happening again. If there was anything to be thankful about in this tragedy, it was that here was the rare case that could lead to tangible reforms, precisely because it involved issues other than grotesque greed and human error. One of the ironies therefore is that so many of the survivors and the families of the dead turned against the JAIC, the only group—however clumsy and alienating—that was responding progressively, and instead found allies among the purely reactive forces, whether Meyer Werft's or Rabe's, who, if they had their way, would allow no changes at all. It was not by chance that

Holtappels's report concluded after several thousand pages without making a single technical recommendation. His point was not that Meyer Werft should continue to make ships as before, but in the abstract, that was the effect.

There were some changes made internationally, largely as a result of the investigation's early findings, during the first year or two, before the reactive forces gained speed and weight. In London the IMO tried to pass a rule that ferries henceforth would have to be able to stay upright with up to a half meter (20 inches) of water on the car deck, but that initiative would have required extensive modifications to ships in service, and it was blocked. Instead, a variety of other regulations were passed, requiring small improvements in stability, stronger bow doors and latches, better monitoring systems (indicator lights and closed-circuit TV), handrails along the escape routes inside, strengthened lower walls along the hallways, better life rafts, better emergency radios, better crew training, and so forth. In IMO terms, this was fairly radical stuff, largely because many of the changes applied not only to new passenger ships but to existing ones. Nonetheless, seven northern European countries were dissatisfied by the rejection of a more stringent damage stability requirement (for water on the car deck), and in 1996 they created one of their own, primarily for ferries sailing the Baltic and the English Channel. The following year, the JAIC issued its final report, which seconded these changes and added some recommendations on top, most notably that strict standards should be applied to independently built ship (bow) components; that the relative responsibilities between shipyard, shipowner, "classification society," and governmental regulators should be formally decided upon; that technical weather limitations and procedures should be established for every ferry, based on the original design; and that all existing passenger vessels should be reevaluated (and if necessary rebuilt) to allow for evacuation. These were fine ideas, but by then they came across like whimpers. Holtappels was on the rise, drumming up support among the crowds, holding his Stockholm "exhibitions." Rabe was starting to spread her poisons. And the JAIC had lost whatever political weight it once had. It turned in its report and disbanded, not because the job was done, but because it was left with no choice. Its investigation had been undermined.

As a result, important questions remain today, pertaining particularly to the ship's final moments as it lay hesitating on its side—the progression the flooding might have taken through the superstructure and then down the stairways and shafts through the central casing, past the flooded car deck, to the lower decks. Specific answers to these questions could provide for delay and even indefinite survival the next time a ferry capsizes. Karppinen wanted to explore these details during the investigation, but could not, for lack of time and resources and access to sufficiently sophisticated computational models. He formed a rough theory that seems about right, but because of ongoing claims about a hole in the starboard hull, his thinking is vigorously disputed. Some modeling has been done by others over the past few years, but rapidly and inconclusively—and, because this is the *Estonia*, with rancor. Further dives on the wreck would certainly help to provide data, but the Swedish government, which tries to exercise control over the wreck, vigorously resists any such intrusions. It is not hiding the truth, as Rabe believes, but has been harassed to the point of disgust. Rolf Sörman for one can sympathize, and though he continues to hope for clear technical answers, he recognizes that the waters he survived now swirl with eddies of distrust.

Six

ON THE BEACH

Captain Vivek A. Pandey thought he could have been a fighter pilot. Because his father had flown for the British before Indian independence, Pandey felt he had flying in his blood. When he was a young man, he took the Indian pilot's aptitude test and astonished the examiners with his spatial orientation, his instinct for flight instruments, and the sureness of his reactions. They saw what he already knew—that he was born with the cool. So when he went to sea, he was not running away, but making a choice. He explained it to me with a rhyme, "from aviation to navigation," as if the two were nearly the same. For seventeen years afterward Pandey plowed the oceans in cargo ships and tankers, under many flags. He became a captain and lived aboard his vessels in master's quarters, some of which seemed to him as luxurious as hotel suites. He visited Norfolk, Savannah, Long Beach, and all the big ports of Europe. He liked the tidiness and power of a ship's command, but eventually he got married and felt the pull of domesticity. And so, thirteen years ago, after the birth of a daughter, he settled in the state of Gujarat, on India's far western shore.

I found him there, in the black hours before a winter dawn, on a beach called Alang—a shoreline strewn with industrial debris on the oily Gulf of Cambay, part of the Arabian Sea. I'd been warned that Pandey would resent my presence and see me as a meddlesome westerner, but he gave no sign of that. He was a sturdy middle-aged merchant captain wearing clean khakis, sneakers, and a baseball cap. Outwardly, he was a calm, businesslike mariner with a job to do. He stood among a group of diffident, rougher-looking men, some in traditional lungis and turbans, and he accepted their offers to share their coconut meat and tea. He checked his watch. He looked out across the dark sea.

A high tide had raised the ocean's level by thirty feet, bringing the waterline a quarter mile inland and nearly to the top of the beach. In the blackness offshore, two ships lay at anchor, visible only by their masthead lights. The first was a 515-foot general-cargo vessel named the *Pioneer 1*, which hailed from St. Vincent, in the Caribbean. Pandey raised a two-way radio to his lips and, calling himself "Alang Control," said, "Okay, *Pioneer One*, heave up your anchor, heave up your anchor."

The *Pioneer's* captain acknowledged the order in thickly accented English. "Roger. Heave up anchor."

To me Pandey said, "We'll start off." He radioed the ship to turn away from the coast and gather speed. "You make one-six-zero degrees, full ahead. What is your distance from the ship behind you?"

"Six cables, six cables."

"Okay, you make course one-six-zero, full ahead."

The masthead lights began to creep through the night. When the captain reported that the ship was steady on the outbound course, Pandey ordered hard starboard rudder. He said, "Let me know your course every ten degrees."

The answer came back shortly: "One-seven-zero, *Pioneer One*." The turn was under way.

"One-eight-zero, *Pioneer One.*" I had to imagine, because I could not see, that great mass of steel trembling under power and swinging toward the shore in the hands of its crew. The captain called the changing courses with tension in his voice. I got the impression he had not done this before. But Pandey was nonchalant. He gazed at silhouettes of sheds that were at the top of the beach. He sipped his tea. The radio said, "One-nine-zero . . . two-zero-zero . . . two-one-zero."

Pandey began talking about the pilot's aptitude test that he had taken years before. He said, "It's a test for which you can appear only once in your lifetime. Either you have the aptitude to be a pilot or you don't, so it is a onetime course in a lifetime. And very interesting . . ."

"Two-two-zero."

On that test, using mechanical controls, Pandey had kept a dot within the confines of a 1.5-inch moving square. Now, using a handheld radio, he was going to ram the *Pioneer*, a ship with a beam of seventy-five feet, into a plot on the beach merely ninety-eight feet wide. It was presumptuous of him, and he knew it. I admired his cool.

The lights of the ship grew closer. The radio said, "Two-three-zero."

Pandey said, "Okay, Captain, you are ballasting, no?"

"Yes, sir, we are ballasting. Ballasting is going on."

"Very good, please continue."

The numbers counted up. At "three-one-zero," with the *Pioneer* now close offshore, Pandey finally showed some emotion. Raising his voice, he said, "Okay, make three-two-zero, steady her. Okay, now you give maximum revolution, Captain! Give maximum revolution!"

I went down to the water's edge. The *Pioneer* came looming

out of the darkness, thrashing the ocean's surface with its single screw, raising a large white bow wake as it rushed toward the beach. I could make out the figures of men peering forward from the bridge, and the bow. Now the sound of the bow wave, like that of a waterfall, drowned the drumming of the engine. A group of workers who had been standing nearby scattered to safety. Pandey joined me at the water's edge. The *Pioneer* kept coming. It was caught by an inshore current that carried it briefly to the side. Then the keel hit the bottom, and the ship drove hard onto the flooded beach, carried by its weight, slowing under full forward power until the rudder no longer functioned and the hull veered out of control and slid to a halt not a hundred yards from where we stood. Anchors the size of cars rattled down the sides and splashed into the shallows. The engine stopped, the lights switched off in succession from bow to stern, and abruptly the *Pioneer* lay dark and still.

If a ship can be animate, as people say, it was at that moment that the *Pioneer* died. It had been built in Japan in 1971, and had wandered the world under various owners and names—*Cosmos Altair, Zephyrus, Bangkok Navee, Normar Pioneer.* And now, as I stood watching from the beach, it became a ferrous corpse—in Indian law as well as in practice no longer a ship but just a mass of imported steel. The seamen who lingered aboard, probing the dead passageways with their flashlight beams, were waiting for the tide to go out, and then they could lower a rope ladder, climb down the side, and walk away on dry ground. The new owner would have his workers start cutting the corpse in the morning.

I asked Pandey if he found this sad, and he answered emphatically that he did not. He was a powerful state official in a nation of powerful officials: he was the port officer of Alang, a man who rode in a chauffeured car with a state emblem on the hood, and it was important to him to appear rational at all times. But the truth, I thought later, might even be that he enjoyed these ship killings. He told me that during his tenure he had personally directed every one—altogether several thousand by now—and he took me along to his next victim, a small cargo vessel also from the Caribbean, which he had already sent speeding toward its destruction. He was proud of his efficiency. He mentioned a personal record of seven ships in succession. He was Pandey the ace, a champion executioner.

Dawn spread across the gargantuan landscape. Alang, in daylight, was barely recognizable as a beach. It was a narrow, smoke-choked industrial zone six miles long, where nearly two hundred ships stood side by side in progressive stages of dissection, yawning open to expose their cavernous holds, spilling their black innards onto the tidal flats, and submitting to the hands of forty thousand impoverished Indian workers. A roughly paved frontage road ran along the top of the beach, parallel to the ocean. It was still quiet at dawn, although a few battered trucks had arrived early and were positioning themselves for the day's first loads of steel scrap. On the ocean side, the frontage road was lined by the metal fences that defined the upper boundaries of the 183 ship-breaking yards at Alang. The fences joined together into an irregular scrap-metal wall that ran intermittently for most of the beach, and above which the bows of ships rose one after another, like giants emerging from the sea. Night watchmen were swinging the yard gates open now, revealing the individual plots, each demarcated by little flags or other markers stuck into the sand, and heavily cluttered with cut metal and nautical debris. The yards looked nearly the same, except for their little offices, usually just inside the gates. The most marginal yards could afford only flimsy shacks or open-sided shelters. The more successful yards had invested in solid structures, some of concrete, with raised verandas and overhead fans.

The workers lived just across the frontage road, in a narrow shantytown that had no sanitation, and for the most part no power. The shantytown did not have a name of its own. It stretched for several miles through the middle of Alang, and it had a small central business section with a few small grocery stalls and stand-up cafés. It was dusty, tough, and crowded. Unemployment there was high. The residents were almost exclusively men, migrants from the distant states of Orissa and Uttar Pradesh. They toiled under shipyard supervisors, typically from their home states or villages, who dispensed the jobs, generally in return for a cut from the workers' already meager pay. Yet the workers chose to work because the alternatives were worse. Now, in the morning light, they emerged from their shacks by the thousands and moved across the frontage road like an army of the poor. They trudged through the yards' open gates, donned hard hats, picked up crowbars and sledgehammers, and lit crude cutting torches. By eight o'clock, the official start of the workday, they had sparks showering from all the ships nearby, and new black smoke was rising into the distance along the coast.

Metaphorically, Alang is a place where the ocean comes ashore, a Third World industrial zone where labor is cheap and regulation is hardly more than a paper-thin veneer. It is also more simply the final expression of a global business freed from the constraints of nationalism and convention, and determined to extract the last possible worth from ships that have grown impossibly old—a value that is assigned on the global market for scrap steel. That value can be considerable, as much as a million dollars for a vessel the size of the *Pioneer*. No one denies that what happens afterward is a dangerous and polluting process, or that the workers involved are frequently injured and sometimes killed. It is said, however, and not without reason, that this is a necessary function of modern times.

Certainly the growth of this industry has closely paralleled the changes under way at sea. Shipbreaking was performed with cranes and heavy equipment at salvage docks by the big shipyards of the United States and Europe until the 1970s, when labor costs and environmental regulations drove most of the business to the docksides of Korea and Taiwan. Eventually, however, even these entrepreneurial countries started losing interest in the business and gradually decided they had better uses for their shipyards. This meant that the world's shipbreaking business was again up for grabs. In the 1980s, enterprising businessmen in India, Bangladesh, and Pakistan seized the initiative with a simple, transforming idea: to break a ship, they did not need expensive docks and tools; they could just wreck the thing—drive it up onto a beach as they might a fishing boat, and tear it apart by hand. The scrap metal to be had from such an operation could be profitably sold because of the growing need in South Asia for low-grade steel, primarily in the form of ribbed reinforcing rods (rebars) to be used in the construction of concrete walls. These rods, which are generally of poor quality, could be locally produced from the ships' hull plating by small-scale "rerolling mills," of which there were soon perhaps a hundred in the vicinity of Alang alone. From start to finish, the chain of transactions depended on the extent of the poverty in South Asia. There was a vast and fast-growing population of people living close to starvation who would work hard for a dollar or two a day, keep the unions out, and accept injuries and deaths without complaint. Neither they nor the government authorities would dream of making an issue of labor or environmental conditions.

The South Asian industry took about a decade to mature. In 1983 Gujarat state proclaimed Alang its shipbreaking site. It was still a pristine shore known only to a few fishermen, without even a dirt road leading to it. Twenty-two shipbreakers leased plots and disposed of five small ships that year. The following year, they disposed of fifty-one. The boom began in the early 1990s as the richer countries of East Asia continued to withdraw from the business.

Today roughly 90 percent of the world's annual crop of seven hundred condemned ships end their lives on the beaches of Pakistan, India, and Bangladesh—and fully half of them die at Alang. With few exceptions, the breakers are not highborn or educated men. They are shrewd traders who have fought their way up; even those who have grown rich have never lost the poor man's feeling of vulnerability. They have good reason to feel insecure. With the most modest of labor costs, shipbreaking is still a marginal business that uses borrowed money and generates slim profits. The risk of failure for even the most experienced breakers is real. Some go under every year. For their workers the risks are worse: falls, fires, explosions, and exposure to a variety of poisons from fuel oil, lubricants, paints, wiring, insulation, and cargo slop. Many workers are killed every year. Nonetheless, by local standards the industry has been a success. Even the lowliest laborers are proud of what they do at Alang. There is no ship too big to be torn apart this way. More important, the economic effects are substantial. Alang and the industries that have sprung from it provide a livelihood, however meager, for perhaps as many as a million Indians. Imagine, therefore, their confusion and anger that among an even greater number of rich and powerful foreigners, primarily in northern Europe, Alang has also become a rallying cry for reform—a name now synonymous with Western complicity and Third World hell.

Captain Pandey by daylight was less in control than he had seemed at night. He appeared tired, even fragile. We stood on the beach among the immense steel carcasses. I brought up the subject of the international campaign, led by Greenpeace in Amsterdam, to reform the process of ship scrapping worldwide. Although global in theory, the campaign in practice is directed mostly against the biggest operation—the beach here at Alang. I had been told that Pandey took the campaign as a personal attack, and indeed, at the mention of Greenpeace he struggled visibly to maintain his composure. His face grew tight and angry. He spoke emphatically, as if to keep from raising his voice. Very clearly he said, "The purposeful propaganda against this yard should be countered. You come and look at the facts, and I'm proud of what I have done over here. So there is nothing to hide." He sounded secretive anyway. He implied that a cabal of shadowy forces was conspiring against Alang and that the real purpose of the environmentalists' campaign was to take the shipbreaking business away from India. He said, "I can show them ten thousand other places outside India, point them out, which are in even worse condition than this. Why should they talk about my country alone?"

Pandey had given his squadron of uniformed guards strict orders to turn away any foreigners trying to enter the yards through the main gate, but determined foreigners kept slipping in anyway. They worked for environmental and human-rights groups and took photographs of black smoke and red fire, and of emaciated workers covered in oil—strong images that, Pandey felt, did not represent a balanced view of Alang. The moral superiority implied by these missions was galling to many Indians, especially here on the sacred ground of Gujarat, the birth state of Mahatma Gandhi. Recently Greenpeace activists had painted slogans on the side of a condemned ship. Pandey must have taken a special pleasure in running that ship aground.

He was a complex man. He claimed to know that he couldn't have it both ways, that he couldn't invite the world's ships to Alang and at the same time expect to keep the world out. Yet he insisted on trying. After the sun rose, he took me to his office. He wanted to stop me from wandering through the yards, and then he escorted me away from Alang entirely, because he wanted to make sure I was gone. I did not mention that I had already been at Alang for more than a week, or that I knew a side road to the site and intended to return.

The controversy over Alang started on the other side of the world and a few years back, in Baltimore, Maryland, along the ghostly industrial shoreline of the city's outer harbor, where old highway signs warn motorists about heavy smoke that no longer pours from the stacks. Early in 1996 a *Baltimore Sun* reporter named Will Englund was out on the water when he noticed a strange sight—the giant aircraft carrier *Coral Sea* lying partially dismantled beside a dock, "in a million pieces." Englund looked into the situation and discovered that the *Coral Sea* was a waterfront fiasco of bankruptcy, lawsuits, worker injuries, toxic spills, and outright criminality. Of particular interest to Baltimore, where thousands of shipyard workers had been disabled by asbestos, was evidence of wholesale exposure once again to that dangerous dust. The U.S. Navy, which still owned the hull, was guilty, it seemed, at least of poor oversight. Englund's first report ran as a front-page story in April 1996. The *Sun's* chief editor, John Carroll, then decided to go after the subject in full. He brought in his star investigative reporter, Gary Cohn, a quick-witted man who had the sort of street smarts that could complement Englund's more cerebral style.

The two reporters worked on the story for more than a year. Their investigation centered on the United States, where shipbreaking had become a nearly impossible business, for the simple reason that the cost of scrapping a ship correctly was higher than the value of its steel. The only reason any remnant of the domestic industry still existed was that since 1994, all government-owned ships—demilitarized navy warships as well as decrepit merchant vessels culled from the nation's mothballed "reserve fleet" by the U.S. Maritime Administration—had been kept out of the overseas scrap market as a result of an Environmental Protection Agency ban against the export of polychlorinated biphenyls, the hazardous compounds known as PCBs, which were used in ships' electrical and hydraulic systems. In practice, the export ban did not apply to the much-larger number of U.S.-flagged commercial vessels that were (and are still) exported freely for overseas salvage. Hoping somehow to make the economics work, American scrappers bought the government ships (or the scrapping rights) at giveaway prices, tore into them as expediently as possible, and in most cases went broke anyway. As a result of these defaults, the Defense Department was forced to repossess many of the vessels that it had awarded to U.S. contractors. Conditions in the remaining yards were universally abysmal. The problems existed nationwide—in California, Texas, North Carolina, and, of course, Maryland. Englund and Cohn were surprised by the lack of previous reporting, and they were fascinated by the intensity of the individual stories—of death or injury in hot, black holds, of environmental damage, and of repeated lawbreaking and cover-ups. Cohn especially was used to working in the underbelly of society, but not even he had imagined that abuses on such a scale could still exist in the United States. When I asked him if he had been motivated by anger or moral outrage, he mulled over the question, then answered, "I don't know that it was so much *anger*. I think we discovered a lot of things that were wrong and needed correcting. But I wouldn't say that we walked around angry all the time." Nonetheless, the subject became their obsession.

At the same time that Cohn and Englund were investigating the story, the U.S. Navy and the Maritime Administration, faced with a growing backlog of rotting hulls, were pressuring the EPA to lift its export ban. They wanted the freedom to sell government ships for a profit on the South Asian scrap market. Englund and Cohn realized that their investigation required a visit to the place where many of these ships would end up if the ban were lifted— a faraway beach called Alang.

The *Sun* enlisted a photographer, hired an Indian stringer to help with logistics, and in February 1997 sent the team to India.

Alang was still an innocent place: the reporters were free to go where they pleased, to take pictures openly, and to pay no mind to Captain Pandey. The reporters were shocked by what they saw. To them Alang was mostly a place of death, and they were not entirely wrong. Soon after they left Alang, sparks from a cutting torch ignited the residual gases in a tanker's hold and caused an explosion that killed fifteen workers—or fifty. Alang was the kind of place where people hardly bothered to count.

The *Sun's* shipbreaking report hit the newsstands for three days in December 1997. It concentrated first on the navy's failures inside the United States and then on Alang. A little storm broke out in Washington. The Maryland senator Barbara A. Mikulski promptly pronounced herself "appalled" and requested a Senate investigation into the navy's conduct. She called simultaneously for the EPA's export ban to stay in place and for an overhaul of the domestic program to address the labor and environmental issues brought up by the *Sun* articles. Though Mikulski spoke in stern moral terms, what she apparently also had in mind was the creation of a new Baltimore jobs program involving the clean, safe, and therefore expensive disposal of ships, to be funded in some way by the federal government. The navy had been embarrassed by the *Sun's* report and was in no position to counter Mikulski's attack. It answered weakly that it welcomed discussions "to ensure [that] the complex process of ship disposal is conducted in an environmentally sound manner and in a way that protects the health and safety of workers." Mikulski shot back a letter to Secretary of Defense William Cohen: "Frankly, I was disappointed in their tepid comments. We don't need hollow promises and clichés. We need an action plan and concrete solutions."

Her opinion was shared by other elected officials in struggling seaports. The Maryland representative Wayne T. Gilchrest announced that his maritime subcommittee would hold hearings. The California representative George Miller said, "I feel strongly that contributing to the pollution and labor exploitation found at places like Alang, India, is not a fitting end for these once-proud ships." Miller also argued that since the navy was paying the cleanup costs at its old bases, it should pay for the scrapping of its old ships as well. It made sense. Certainly the U.S. government could afford it.

In the last days of 1997 the navy surrendered, declaring that it was suspending plans to export its ships. Reluctantly the Maritime Administration agreed to do the same. The government had a backlog of 170 ships awaiting destruction, with others scheduled to join them. Faced with the continuing decay of those ships—and the possibility that some of them would soon sink—the Defense Department formed an interagency shipbreaking panel and gave it two months to report back with recommendations. The panel suffered from squabbling, but it dutifully went through the motions of deliberation.

During a public hearing in March 1998, the speakers made just the sort of dull and self-serving statements one would expect. Ross Vincent, of the Sierra Club, said, "Waste should be dealt with where it is generated."

George Miller said, "A global environmental leader like the United States should not have as a national policy the exporting of its toxic waste to developing countries ill equipped to handle it."

Barbara Mikulski said, "We ought to take a look at how we can turn this into an opportunity for jobs in our shipyards."

Stephen Sullivan, of Baltimore Marine Industries, said, "We have a singular combination of shipbuilding, ship-conversion, and ship-repair expertise."

And Murphy Thornton, of the shipbuilders union, said, "Those ships should be buried with honor."

In April 1998 Englund and Cohn won the Pulitzer Prize for investigative reporting. That same month, the shipbreaking panel issued its final report—a bland document that reflexively called for better supervision of the domestic industry and wistfully maintained the hope of resuming exports, but it also suggested that a navy pilot project explore the costs of clean ship disposal in the United States. By September 1999 an appropriation had moved through Congress, and the future finally seemed clear: the "pilot project" included only 4 out of 180 ships, but it involved an initial sum of $13.3 million, to be awarded on a "cost-plus" basis to yards in Baltimore, Brownsville, Philadelphia, and San Francisco—and by definition it was just the start.

This was Washington in action. A problem had been identified and addressed through a demonstrably open and democratic process, and a solution had been found that was affordable and probably about right. Nonetheless, there was something wrong about the process—an elusive quality not exactly of corruption, but of a repetitive and transparent dishonesty that seemed to imply either that the public was naïve or that it could not be trusted with straight talk. Even the *Baltimore Sun* had joined in: in September 1998, when then–Vice President Al Gore went through the motions of imposing another (redundant) ban on exports, an approving *Sun* editorial claimed that the prohibition "especially benefits the poorly paid and untrained workers in the wretched shipyards of South Asia." Patently absurd assertions like that may help to explain why shipbreaking reform, despite all the trappings of a public debate—including coverage in the national press and even ultimately the Pulitzer Prize—actually attracted very little attention in the United States. The people who might naturally have spared this issue a few moments of thought may have had little patience for the rhetoric. Or maybe the subject just seemed too small and far away. For whatever reason, the fact is that the American public did not notice the linguistic nicety distinguishing the government ships in question from the larger number of commercial U.S.-flagged ships that would remain untouched by the reforms. So an argument about double standards, which should at least have been heard, was expediently ignored. Seen from outside the United States, the pattern was hard to figure out. India, of course, paid attention to the controversy. At Alang, where plenty of American commercial vessels still came to die, people couldn't understand why the U.S. government's ships were banned. I could never quite bridge the cultural gap to explain the logic. How does one say that the process had simply become an exercise in democracy from above? A subject had been tied off and contained.

Tied off and contained in America, that is. As it turned out, the *Sun's* exposé did affect Alang, but in a way that no one in Washington had anticipated. The surprise came close on the heels of the Pulitzer Prize, when the hellish image of Alang landed hard in Scandinavia and the countries of the Rhine, where it ignited a popular movement for shipbreaking reform. It might seem unlikely that ordinary people would genuinely care about a problem so abstract and far away; nevertheless, in northern Europe millions of them did. In The Hague, a typically progressive Dutch official explained to me that his countrymen had less frantic lives than Americans and could spare the time for altruism.

The campaign, which continues today, was led from Greenpeace's global headquarters in Amsterdam by plainspoken activists who started in where American reformers hadn't ventured—going after the big commercial shipping lines. By spring of 2000 the activists had muscled their way into the maritime lawmaking forums and had begun to threaten the very existence of Alang.

Their task was made easier from the outset by the work of the emotive Brazilian photojournalist Sebastião Salgado, who came upon the story when it was young, in 1989, and captured unforgettable images of gaunt laborers and broken ships on the beach in Bangladesh. In 1993 Salgado exhibited his photographs at several shows in Europe and in his superb picture book *Workers*, which was widely seen. An awareness of the particular hardships of shipbreaking began to percolate in the European consciousness, as did the suspicion that perhaps somehow a caring West should intervene. Then, in 1995, Greenpeace had a famous brush with marine "salvage" when it discovered that Shell intended to dispose of a contaminated oil-storage platform, the giant Brent Spar, by sinking it in the North Atlantic. Greenpeace boarded the platform, led a consumer boycott against Shell (primarily at gas stations in Germany), and with much fanfare forced the humiliated company to back down. The Brent Spar was towed to a Norwegian fjord and scrapped correctly, an expensive job that continued for years. Greenpeace had once again shown itself to be a powerful player on the European scene.

Greenpeace was powerful because it was popular, and it was popular because it was audacious, imaginative, and incorruptible. It also had a knack for entertaining its friends. When the drama of

Alang came into clear view, Greenpeace recognized the elements for a new campaign. The organization was not being cynical. For many years it had been involved in a fight to stop the export of toxic wastes from rich countries to poor—a struggle that had culminated in an international accord known as the Basel Ban, an export prohibition, now in effect, to which the European Union nations had agreed. Greenpeace considered the Basel Ban an important victory, and it saw the shipbreaking trade as an obvious violation: if the ships were not themselves toxins, they were permeated with toxic materials, and were being sent to South Asia as a form of waste. Greenpeace was convinced that ships owned by companies based in the nations that had signed the accord, no matter what flag those ships flew, were clearly banned from export. It was a good argument. Moreover, the shipping industry's counterargument—that the ships went south as *ships*, becoming waste only after hitting the beaches—provided a nice piece of double-talk that Greenpeace could hold up for public ridicule. And Alang, with its filth and smoke, provided perfect panoramas to bring the point home. So Greenpeace went to war.

It was October 1998, a year and a half after the *Sun's* visit. Captain Pandey was on guard against trouble, but he must have been looking in the wrong direction. A group of Greenpeace activists got onto the beach by posing as shipping buffs interested in the story of a certain German vessel. They said they wanted the ship's wheel. But they also wandered off and took pictures of the squalor, and they scraped up samples from the soil, the rubble, and the shantytown shacks. After analyzing those samples, two German laboratories quantified what Greenpeace already knew—that Alang was powerfully poisonous, particularly for the laborers who worked, ate, and slept at dirt level there. Greenpeace issued the findings in a report, the most comprehensive written on Alang. The report discussed the medical consequences of the contaminants and described the risk of industrial accidents, which were rumored to cause 365 deaths a year. "Every day one ship, every day one dead," went the saying about Alang, and although the report's authors admitted that there was no way to verify this, it was a formulation that people remembered.

Greenpeace needed a culprit to serve as a symbol of the European shipping business, and it found one in the tradition-bound P&O Nedlloyd, an Anglo-Dutch cargo line that was openly selling its old ships on the Asian scrap market. In the shadowy world of shipping, P&O Nedlloyd was a haplessly anchored target: it had a big office building on a street in Rotterdam and a staff of modern middle-class Europeans, altruists who tended to sympathize with Greenpeace and would quietly keep it apprised of P&O Nedlloyd's intentions and movements. Also, because a related company called P&O Cruises operated a fleet of English Channel ferries and cruise ships, P&O Nedlloyd was likely to be sensitive to public opinion. In November 1998 Greenpeace staged a protest at the company's offices, erecting a giant photograph of a scrapped ship at Alang, along with a statement in Dutch: "P&O Nedlloyd burdens Asia with it." The press arrived, and eventually a company director emerged from the building to talk to the activists. He did not appear to be afraid or angry. He said it wasn't fair to single out P&O Nedlloyd, and he made the argument that coordinated international regulation was needed. International regulation was exactly what Greenpeace wanted, but when the next day's paper came out with a photograph captioned "P&O and Greenpeace agree," Greenpeace denied that there had been any understanding.

The truth was that Greenpeace needed resistance from P&O

Nedlloyd, and it would have had to rethink its strategy if the company had submitted to its demands and obediently stopped scrapping in Asia. But of course P&O Nedlloyd did not submit—and, for that matter, could not afford to submit. After its brief attempt at openness, it went into just the sort of sullen retreat that Greenpeace might have hoped for. Greenpeace staged a series of shipside banner unfurlings, and it dogged a doomed P&O Nedlloyd container vessel, appropriately called the *Encounter Bay*, as it went about the world on its final errands. Millions of Greenpeace sympathizers watched with glee. P&O Nedlloyd was so unnerved by the campaign that in the spring of 1999 it painted a new name on a ship bound for the Indian beach, in order, perhaps, to disguise who owned it. Greenpeace found out and shouted in indignation. When P&O Nedlloyd then refused to comment, it began to look like an old man turned to evil. This made for good theater—especially against the backdrop of the ubiquitous pictures of Alang.

With public opinion now fully aroused, the northern European governments began to move, introducing the first dedicated shipbreaking initiatives into the schedules of the European Union and the IMO. In June 1999 the Netherlands sponsored an international shipbreaking conference in Amsterdam—a meeting whose tone was established at the outset by an emotional condemnation of the industry by the Dutch Minister of Transport. It was obvious to everyone there that the movement for reform was gathering strength. It was hard to know what changes would result—and which shipbreaking nations would be affected—but the reformers were ambitious, and their zeal was genuine. If they could not regulate the oceans, or truly affect the business on a global scale, they could at least embarrass India into shutting down Alang. Pandey had reason to be afraid.

In London that fall, I met an affable Englishman named Brian Parkinson, who worked as a trade and operations adviser for the International Chamber of Shipping, an umbrella group of national shipowner associations. Parkinson had a natural appreciation for the anarchy of the sea and an equally natural aversion to the Greenpeace campaign. He said, "Shipping gets blamed for everything. Global warming. Why the British don't have a decent football team." For lunch we went to a dark little pub that should have been on the docks. Parkinson told me that he was near the end of his career and was looking forward to retirement. Meanwhile, however, he was struggling gamely to keep pace with the times. He said, "A ship registered in Panama, owned by a Norwegian, operating in the U.S., and sold in India is *not* an export—but we're not making that argument." He said, "Maybe there *are* things that shipowners can do." First, he had in mind a nice bit of public relations: "We're looking at creating an inventory of hazardous components, a good-housekeeping guide. We want to know how we can present the ship to the recyclers in the best possible way." I complimented him on the word "recyclers," and he said yes, right, it was rather good, wasn't it? But he was toying with something a bit more real as well—a proposal for voluntary self-regulation, under which the industry would inspect and certify the yards at the Asian beaches and then factor in good behavior when choosing which ones to use. He mentioned that Shell had already sent an inspector to a yard at Alang, and this inspector was said to have written an in-house report. As evidence of progress, this seemed pretty slim. I asked Parkinson what was to keep his scheme from becoming a two-tiered arrangement, whereby a few image-conscious companies would accept the expense of working with certified yards while all the other shipowners continued with business as usual, selling their vessels to the highest bidders. He said he worried about that too.

At the central train station in Amsterdam a few days later I met Parkinson's opponent, a leader of the Greenpeace campaign, Claire Tielens, a young Dutch woman with a walker's stride and an absolutist's frank gaze. We went to the station café and talked.

I asked her if she had visited India yet, and she said no, but for several years she had been a reporter for an environmental news service in the Philippines, so she knew about Third World conditions. I said, "Why did you choose Alang? Why does it seem worse to you than the other industrial sites in India?"

She answered, "Because here there is a very direct link with Western companies."

"But if it's Western companies at Alang versus Indian companies somewhere else, what difference does it make to the world's environment?"

"Because those Western companies pretend to us here with glossy leaflets that they are so environmentally responsible. And it is a shame when they export their shit to the developing world."

"But from your environmental point of view," I asked, "what difference does it make who the polluter is and whether he's a hypocrite or not? I mean, what is it about shipbreaking? And what is it about Alang?"

I kept phrasing my questions badly. She kept trying to answer me directly, and failing, and going over the same ground. Without intending to, I was being unfair. She should have said, "We needed to make some choices, and so we chose Alang. It was easy—and look how far we've come." I think that would have been about right. Instead she said, "Even by Indian standards, Alang is bad." But India has a billion people, and it is famously difficult to define.

New Delhi sprawls on dirty ground under ashen skies. It is an immense capital city, a noisy expression of the Indian democracy, not quite the anarchy that at first it appears to be, but a conglomeration of countless private worlds. I found myself there in winter at late-night dinners and garden parties among the city's large middle class—professionals who drove when they might have walked, and who inhabited houses like little forts, with guarded gates and shard-topped walls. They worried about crime—partly, I think, because they could defend against it. The larger assaults on a life in New Delhi were simply overwhelming. A friend of mine with a small trucking company was concerned about the progressive failure of the city's infrastructure and what that meant for his business. He took me to visit New Delhi's chief urban planner, a powerful official who sat defeated at an empty steel desk in a big bare office and out of boredom and loneliness detained us with small talk and offers of tea. After we escaped, my friend said, "It's incredible, no? I wanted you to see this. It's like he's sitting there at the end of the world."

But to me it was the pollution in New Delhi that seemed apocalyptic. The streams were dead channels trickling with sewage and bright chemicals, and the air on the streets was at times barely breathable. In the heat of the afternoons a yellow-white mixture hung above the city, raining acidic soot into the dust and exhaust fumes. At night the mixture condensed into a dry, choking fog that enveloped the headlights of passing cars and crept with its stink into even the tightest houses. The residents could do little to keep the poison out of their lungs or the lungs of their children, and if they were poor, they could not even try. People told me it was taking years off their lives. Yet New Delhi was bursting its seams because newcomers from rural India kept flooding in.

Mumbai has a reputation for being just as dirty, but on the day I got there, an ocean breeze was blowing, and in relative terms the air was clean. When I mentioned this to Pravin S. Nagarsheth, the shipbreaker I had come to see, he grew excited and said, "Yeah! Yeah!" because relativity was precisely the point he wanted to make to me. Nagarsheth was a nervous little man with a round and splotchy face and some missing teeth. He had been scrapping ships for nearly thirty-five years, first with a small yard here in Mumbai, and then in a bigger way at Alang. He was also the president of the Indian shipbreakers' association, and as such he had taken the lead in the industry's defense. He had traveled to the Amsterdam shipbreaking conference to counter the reports of abuses at Alang. In his speech there he said, "All these write-ups, I would say, are biased, full of exaggerations . . . One, however, wonders whether such reports are deliberately written for public consumption in affluent Western societies only . . . The environmentalists and Greenpeace talk of future generations, but are least bothered about the plight of the present generation. Have they contributed anything constructive to mitigate the plight of the people living below the poverty line in developing countries? . . . Living conditions of labor in Alang should not be looked at in isolation. It is the crisis of urbanization due to job scarcity. Large-scale slums have mushroomed in all cities . . . The fact remains that workers at Alang are better paid and are probably safer than their counterparts back in the poor provinces of Orissa, Bihar, and Uttar Pradesh. To provide housing and better living conditions . . .

is financially impractical for a developing country like India, where 45 percent of the population is living below the poverty line."

We met in the lobby of a shabby hotel in central Mumbai. Nagarsheth kept leaning into me, grabbing my arm to punctuate his arguments. He said, "Everybody knows this is bad! It is not a point of dispute! What Greenpeace is saying is even excellent! But their ideology does not provide solutions! This generation cannot afford it!"

Nagarsheth seemed to worry that I would understand the country in some antiseptic way—for its computer industry, its novelists, or maybe even its military might. But the India he wanted me to see was a place that related directly to Alang, an India drowning in the poverty of its people. And so, rather than talking anymore about shipbreaking, he insisted on showing me around Mumbai. He guided me into the city's slums, which are said to be the largest in the world. Then he led me back toward the city center, for miles through a roadside hell where peasants lived wall to wall in scrap boxes and shacks, and naked children sat listless in the traffic's blue smoke as if waiting to die. Nagarsheth said, "Do you see this? Do you see this? You need to remember it when you get to Alang."

He was making a valid point about relative levels of misery. I saw another level a few days later, in Bhavnagar, the nearest city to Alang, at a rerolling mill where hull plates from the ships were being torch cut, heated, and stretched into reinforcing bars. Bhavnagar is an uncrowded city by Indian standards, with a population of perhaps six hundred thousand in a physical shell that to a westerner might seem better suited for a fourth of that. The rerolling mill I visited was one of many there. It stood on the north edge of town, on a quiet dirt street wandered by cows, at the end of a crumbling brick wall, beyond the dust and din of the city's auto-rickshaws. The mill had a sagging iron gate. A traveler would normally pass it by, perhaps seeing it as a poor but peaceful scene. But I went inside, past an old brick building where clerks sat idle behind bulky typewriters on an outside porch, and on into the dark heart of the mill—a large open-sided shed where perhaps a hundred emaciated men moved through soot and heavy smoke, feeding scrap to a roaring furnace leaking flames from cracks in the side. The noise was deafening. The heat was so intense that in places I thought it might sear my lungs. The workers' clothes were black with carbon, as were their hair and their skin. Their faces were so sooty that their eyes seemed illuminated.

The furnace was long and low. The men working closest to the fire tried to protect themselves by wrapping thick rags around their mouths and legs. They cut the steel plates into heavy strips, which they heaved into the inferno and dragged through the furnace before wrestling them free, red-hot, at the far end. Using long tongs, they slung the smoking metal, still brightly glowing, through a graduated series of rollers that squeezed and lengthened it incrementally into the final product—the reinforcing rods, which were piled together and allowed to cool. It was a punishing and dangerous procedure, requiring agility, strength, and speed, and also the calculation of risk. The workers were obviously exhausted by it. Some, I think, were slowly starving, trapped in that cycle of nutritional deficit all too common in South Asia, by which a man may gradually expend more calories on his job than his wages will allow him to replace.

I traveled from Bhavnagar to Alang, thirty miles to the south, on a narrow road crowded with jitneys and trucks, choked with blue exhaust, and battered by the weight of steel scrap. The road ran like an industrial artery across plains of denuded farmland, on which impoverished villages endured in torpor and peasants scratched at the parched earth. Along the way stood a few open-air cafés, where truck drivers could stop for soft drinks and food, and a few small factories, where oxygen was concentrated into steel bottles to be mixed later with cooking gas for use in the cutting operations farther south. But otherwise the roadside scenery remained agricultural until several miles before Alang. There, next to a small house on the right, a collection of lifeboats listed in the dirt. The lifeboats marked the start of Alang's roadside market-place, where specialized traders neatly sorted and resold secondary merchandise from the ships. There were yards for generators, motors, transformers, kitchen appliances, beds and other furniture, wires and pipes, cables, ropes, life rings, clothing, industrial fluids, and miscellaneous machinery. The traders lived among their goods. The buyers came from all over India.

The marketplace continued for several miles to Alang's main gate. But the best way to the beach for a westerner, given Captain Pandey's concerns about foreigners, was a small side road that branched off a few miles before the main gate and wandered again through rural scenery. I passed a boy herding cows, three women carrying water, a turbaned farmer hoeing. The heat was oppressive. The air smelled of dung and dust. For a while it was almost possible to forget that the ocean was near. But then the road made a turn, and at the far end of a field an immense cargo ship rose above the trees. Behind it, fainter and in the haze, stood another. The ships seemed to emerge from the earth, as if the peasants had found a way to farm them.

My base at the beach was Plot 138. It was a busy patch of ground, bounded at the top by one of the standard sheet-metal fences. I threaded through piles of sorted scrap, past the smoke of cutting crews, past chanting gangs carrying heavy steel plate, past cables and chains and roaring diesel winches, to the water's edge, where the hulk of a 466-foot Japanese-built cargo ship called the *Sun Ray*, once registered in the Maldives, was being torn apart by an army of the poor. Four hundred men worked there, divided into three distinct groups—a shipboard elite of cutters and their assistants, who were slicing the hull into multi-ton pieces; a ground crew of less experienced men, who winched those pieces partway up the beach and reduced them there to ten-foot sections of steel plate; and, finally, the masses of unskilled porters condemned to the end of the production line, where, piece by piece, they would eventually shoulder the entire weight of the hull, lugging the heavy plates to the upper beach and loading them into trucks—belching monsters painted like Hindu shrines—that would haul the scrap away. And that was just for the steel. Everywhere I looked stood piles of secondary products awaiting disposal—barrels of oil and hydraulic fluid and all the assorted equipment destined for the roadside marketplace. In either direction, I could look down the coast at a line of torn ships fading into the smoke of burning oil.

Alang at first is a scene of complete visual confusion. It begins to make sense only after about a week, when the visual impact fades and the process of breaking a ship by hand sorts itself out into a series of simple, brutal activities. The first job is to shackle the ship more firmly to the ground. Using motorized winches and a combination of anchor chains and braided steel cables looped through holes cut into the bow, the workers draw the hull as high onto the beach as the ship's draft and trim allow, so that ideally the bow stands on dry ground even at high tide. The winches are diesel-powered machines, each the size of a small bulldozer, staked firmly to the ground about halfway up the beach. The stress on the cables during the winching operation is enormous. They groan and clank under the load, and sometimes they snap dangerously. The workers are ordered to stand clear. Nonetheless, some winch operators sit unprotected by safety cages and gamble that a broken cable will never recoil directly back at them. It's easy to imagine that sometimes they lose.

After the initial dragging is done, the crews climb aboard with ladders and ropes and begin to empty the ship's fuel tanks: they pump the good oil into barrels for resale and slop the residual sludge of no commercial value onto dry ground, where it is burned. The empty tanks continue to produce volatile vapors and pose a risk of explosion until they are aerated—a tricky process that often involves cutting ventilation holes. The most experienced cutters are used for this work because they are believed to have developed noses for dangerous vapors. Even so, there are explosions and fatalities, though fewer now than before, because of slowly improving techniques. On some ships the tanks can be sliced off whole, dropped into the water, and winched above the tide line for dissection and disposal. Cutting on hard ground is easier than cutting on the ship, and because the workers are therefore more likely to do the job right, it is also safer. But either way, the yard must demonstrate to Gujarat officials that the fuel tanks have been secured and neutralized before they will give the final authorization to proceed with the scrapping.

With the risk of explosion diminished, the breakers turn their attention to the ship's superstructure, the thin-walled quarters that typically rise five or six levels above the main deck, in which, because of combustible wiring and wood paneling, the chance of a deadly fire cannot be ignored. The superstructure is like a ghost town, still full of the traces of its former inhabitants. Scattered about are old books and magazines in various languages, nautical charts from faraway oceans, company manuals, years' worth of ship's logs, newspaper clippings, national flags, signal flags, radio frequency lists, union pamphlets, letters, clothes, posters, and sometimes a much-appreciated stock of liquor, narcotics, or pornography. The scrappers spread through the quarters like hungry scavengers, quickly removing the furniture and galley equipment, tearing into the wood paneling and asbestos insulation to get at the valuable plumbing, stripping out the wires, electronics, and instruments, and making a special effort to save the ship's bell, always in demand for use at Hindu temples. These treasures are roped down the side and hustled to the top of the beach by ground crews.

Then the cutting begins. It is surprising how few men are needed to handle the torches: by working simultaneously on the port and starboard sides, a dozen competent cutters, backed up by a larger number of assistants, can demolish an entire superstructure within two weeks. Gravity helps. Starting with the overhanging wings of the bridge, the cutters slice the superstructure into big sections. There is an art to this, because every ship is different. The decisions about where to cut are made by the yard's owner and the all-important shipboard supervisor. Within the logical demolition sequence (which with variations runs roughly from front to back and from top to bottom) the general idea is to cut off the largest section that can be cleared away from the ship by the shore-based winches. The height and geometry of the superstructure is a crucial consideration because it affects the way the sections fall. If the work has been done right, when the final cut on a section is made, it falls clear of the hull. It lands on the tidal flat with a dull thump. The ground crew walks out to it, attaches a cable, and winches it higher onto the beach to carve it up. Meanwhile, the shipboard crews may already have dropped another section. At this early stage it can be gratifying work. If the superstructure is flimsy, the crews can make the metal rain.

But the work slows when they come to the hull, where the steel is heavier and harder to cut. At that point, even for veteran workers, there must be a moment of hesitation at the audacity of the business. Using little more than cooking gas and muscle power, they will tear apart this immense monolith that towers above the crowds on the sand. It will take six months or a year to finish the job; men will be injured, and some may die. Almost all will to some degree be poisoned by smoke and toxic substances—more seriously, no doubt, than they would have been on the streets of India's cities. Nonetheless, the poor cannot afford to be timid.

They go after the hull by cutting off the forward section of the bow, opening the ship's cavernous forward hold to the outside, and making room for an expanded force of shipboard cutting crews. Half of them continue to cut at the forward section, slowly moving aft; the other half burrow directly back through the ship, cutting away the internal bulkheads until they come to the engine room, near the stern. The ship's engine is not usually saved, because generally it is worn out, and in any case it is often too large to be removed whole. The crews open ventilation holes through the sides of the hull, unbolt the engine, disconnect it from the shafts, and cut it apart crudely on the spot. They drag the pieces forward through the length of the ship with the help of small winches placed aboard for that purpose.

To understand why it is important to remove the engine early, consider that the ship continues in part to float throughout the scrapping process and that high tides lift it, allowing the progressive winchings by which, as the hull is consumed, it is drawn onto the beach. From the start, the ship's trim is a consideration. If the angle at which the keel is floating does not match the slope of the ocean floor, the ship may hang up offshore. The trick is not to get the bow to ride high, as one might assume, but rather to keep the stern of an unladen ship from riding too low. The stern naturally rides low because of the weight of the superstructure, the engine, and the machinery installed there. Once the scrapping is under way, the correct trim can be maintained only by the judicious removal of weight. Cutting away the superstructure and removing the heavy bronze propeller does not fully compensate for the subsequent loss of the bow section, whose weight, because it lies so far forward of the ship's center of gravity, has a disproportionate effect on the trim. That is why the breakers must go in from the opened bow and take out the engine. Afterward the demolition proceeds so predictably, from bow to stern, that it is possible to mark its conclusion precisely when the ship's rudder lies at last on dry ground, submitting to the torches. The workers do not celebrate the achievement, because if they are lucky, the next ship has already arrived.

Plot 138, the yard that I settled into, was the domain of Paras Ship Breakers Ltd., a company owned by a man named Chiman Bai, who began his career as an errand boy in the ancient Bhavnagar market and rose to become a shopkeeper selling rice and wheat. Bai got into the shipbreaking business in 1983, when he responded to an obscure notice in the newspaper about the availability of plots at Alang. I never met him, I think because he felt awkward with foreigners. It was said that he still worked from a

back office in the market and that he presided over an extended
family of thirty-five, all of whom lived in a single house in Bhavnagar and ate their meals together in the traditional way, sitting on
the kitchen floor. His younger brother, Jaysukh Bai, ran the shipbreaking operation day to day. He was a square-jawed, gray-
haired man with a Hindu cloth bracelet and a diamond ring. He
did business at an office in Bhavnagar every morning, and in the
afternoon he made his way to Alang, where he sat among his sons
and nephews on a porch overlooking the yard. I sat with him
sometimes, drinking the Indian cola called Thumbs Up, breathing
the acrid smoke from the final cutting of ship parts, some of which
was done nearby. Jaysukh Bai did not seem to notice the smoke.
One of his nephews figured that I did. He distrusted me and repeatedly made that clear. Once he said nastily, "The question I
want to ask the environmentalists is if you should want to die first
of starvation or pollution."

I said, "They say you don't have to make that choice."

He said, "That's bullshit."

In a place like Alang, he was probably right.

Sometimes I wandered across the road into the crowded shantytown where the workers lived, a place with shacks built of wood
and ships' paneling, some on stilts over a malarial marsh that bor-
dered the beach. There were no latrines at Alang, in part because
few of the men would have used them. They preferred simply to
relieve themselves in nearby bushes, as they had in the farming
hamlets from which they came. But of course Alang was much
larger than a hamlet, and as a result the air there was filled with fe-
cal odors, which mixed with the waves of smoke and industrial
dust to permeate the settlement with a potent stench. People got
used to it, as they did to the mosquitoes and the flies. Discomfort

was an accepted part of living in Alang, as was disease. Thousands of workers who were sick, injured, or unemployed lingered in the shantytown during the day, lying on scavenged linoleum floors by open doorways, or sitting outside in the thin shade of the walls. There were almost no wives or children. As in other migrant camps, drunkenness, prostitution, and violence were never far away.

Nonetheless, a semblance of normalcy was maintained. For instance, Alang had a good drinking-water system, a network of communal cisterns supplied by truck, which was Captain Pandey's pride. It also had Hindu shrines, informal cricket fields, and enough spare power for its commercial district to run refrigerators and gay little strings of lights. Each evening when the workday was done, the settlement came to life. The workers cooked outside their shacks in small groups, intent on the food, and afterward, feeling renewed, they gathered in the light from the cafés and talked. They laughed. They listened to music. Sometimes they held religious processions. Sometimes they danced. And then on Sundays, when by law all the shipbreaking yards were closed, they washed, dressed up, and strolled among friends, looking fresh and clean-cut.

One evening a small group from Plot 138 invited me to sit with them outside their shack, and one of them went off into the slum and came back with a man who could translate. It was awkward for everyone. The men were formal with me. I asked about their work. They knew it was risky and could make them sick, but they seemed more interested in letting me know that they were cutters and that they stood high on the scrap-yard scale. I asked about their bosses, and they named some of the supervisors who had given them jobs. They said that in other yards some of the supervisors were abusive. They offered no opinions about Jaysukh Bai, maybe because they had seen me with him.

After a week, Pravin Nagarsheth arrived from Mumbai to check on his shipyard, a few plots down from Plot 138. A ship lay there half consumed on the beach. Nagarsheth brought his son-in-law with him, a slim city boy in undersized Ray-Bans who slipped carefully around the workers and confided to me, "The first time I came here, I was totally zapped." He meant he was surprised. He seemed a bit precious. But Nagarsheth was not like that, and neither was Jaysukh Bai. They were direct men who walked willingly among their laborers; and though they had grown wealthy on the backs of the poor, they had maintained a connection to them nonetheless. The alternative seemed to be the disengagement I had witnessed in New Delhi and Mumbai, where the upper levels of society were floating free of the ground, aided by the airlines and the Internet, as if the poverty in India were a geographic inconvenience. Nagarsheth's own daughter had graduated from the University of Chicago with a degree in computer science, and he was proud of her. But standing beside him on the beach, in the midst of his piles of scrap, I suspected he knew that shipbreakers were unfashionable among the Indian elites. He may even have been able to see himself as they did—an angry little man with a propensity for mucking around in the world's garbage. In the foreign press I had discerned an undertone of mockery about such things, a vestige of the old colonial amusement at the very idea of native kings. Even the *Baltimore Sun* had indulged in the fun, quoting an interior decorator from Mumbai who ridiculed the flamboyant tastes on exhibit in the shipbreakers' big houses in Bhavnagar. Such public amusement was of course noticed elsewhere in India, especially among the ruling classes, who were so successfully joining the "global" (meaning Westernized) society. Now, in Mumbai and New Delhi, a young and soon to be powerful generation was returning from European and American universities speaking the language of environmentalism. And Alang was becoming an embarrassment.

Alang has become a metaphor in the crucial struggle of our time—that between the First World and the Third, the rich and the poor. In a slightly different form, it is the same struggle that plays out on the open ocean. Beneath our perspectives on a shrinking world lurks an opposing reality, hidden in the poverty of places like South Asia, of a world that is becoming larger, and unmanageably so. Do we share a global ecology? On a certain level it's obvious that we do and that therefore a genuine scientific argument can be made for the imposition of Western knowledge and sensitivities. But making this argument is difficult, full of political risk and the opportunity for self-delusion. In practice, the world is as much a human construct as a natural one. The people who inhabit it have such radically different experiences in life that it can be almost surprising that they share the same air. This is inherently hard to accept from a distance. Too often we have a view of what is desirable for some other part of the world—on the ocean, in the slums from which sailors come, in Alang—which is so detached from daily existence there that it becomes counterproductive, or even inhumane. At Alang, resentful Indians kept saying to me, "You had your industrial revolution, and so we should have ours." I kept suggesting in return that history is not so symmetrical. But of course they knew that already. They viewed Alang, and the ocean itself, with more complexity than they could express to me, and were using a simplified argument they felt I might understand. On the ship-scrapping beach at Chittagong, in

Bangladesh, I met an angry man who took the simplest approach. He said, "You are sitting on top of the World Trade Center, sniffing fresh air, and talking about it. You don't know anything." And then, of course, the World Trade Center came falling down.

The man in Bangladesh was angry about the West's presumptuousness and its strength. He was angry about people like Claire Tielens at Greenpeace. When I talked to Tielens in Amsterdam, she was absolute and unyielding about Greenpeace's demands. She said, "Ships should not be scrapped in Asia unless they are decontaminated and they don't contain toxic materials. New ships should be built in such a way that they can be scrapped safely—so without hazardous materials if possible. The export of toxin-containing ships from Western countries to developing countries should be stopped. And if possible, ships should be cleaned throughout their lifetime. If they export clean steel, that's fine with us."

I said, "But ships will always contain toxic wastes. Is it economically possible to . . ."

"Economically? Well, of course that's a very flexible term."

But the economics are less flexible than she believed. One of the twists in this story is that the U.S. government, an entity that Greenpeace has a prerogative to dislike, has become without question the world's most principled shipowner, and as such is leading the way in establishing the real costs of doing things right. I spent an afternoon at an anchorage run by the Maritime Administration on the James River in Virginia, climbing through floating wrecks among the ever-growing number of government derelicts awaiting a proper domestic disposal. On one ship a workman had painted SINK ME! as a way of tempting fate. All these ships were rusting through. The annual costs for routine monitoring, pumping, and patching amounted to an average of about $20,000 per vessel. That may not seem like much, but many of the hulls were in such poor condition that to keep them from sinking, they would soon have to be dry-docked for million-dollar repairs—only to be towed back to their moorings to continue rusting. The ships could now be bought for a mere $10 each, but even at that price there were no takers. At the Maritime Administration's headquarters, in Washington, D.C., people recognized the absurdity of the situation and could laugh about it. All they could do was hope for congressional funding to pay for the scrapping of the ships.

Meanwhile, the navy was proceeding with its four-ship, $13.3 million pilot project. Dockside at Baltimore Marine Industries the next day, I visited a small frigate named the *Patterson* that was being meticulously dismantled by a crew of fifty-four specialists working under the close supervision of a former navy diver who informed me, when I asked about the schedule and cost, that safety and a clean environment were his main concerns. His ship had space-suited workers, positive-pressure filtered ventilation, sealed hazardous-materials bins, color-coded placards, and micron socks hanging from the scuppers to purify the rainwater that drained from its immaculate decks. I realized I was in the presence of a shipbreaking pioneer. This man understood the ethical need to spend millions more on a useless ship than its steel was worth. He consulted with chemists, liaison people, and all sorts of engineers. He shared information openly with his competitors, and expected them to do the same. He enforced a wide range of regulations, and fairly. He worked well with unions. He even took time to respect the memory of the *Patterson*'s sailors. His shipbreaking mission was so righteous it was practically Calvinistic.

That was true of Greenpeace's mission too. But there was a strange reversal. The U.S. Navy for once was concentrating on its own local problem, while Greenpeace was insisting that it had a mandate from "the global society" and "citizens of this planet." Words like those can come across as direct threats of a reconquest by the West—all the more so on ships at sea, or in weak and uncertain places like the impoverished parts of India that are already suffering from the disengagement of the elites.

I don't think Claire Tielens worried about such sensitivities. She told me that she had chosen her path because she wanted to fight injustice. She was a true idealist. But she did not feel reluctant to say, "The recycling of toxic waste is such a hazardous activity that you cannot leave it to a developing country to do that. People say, 'Why don't we export our knowledge and technology, and they can improve their conditions, and everything will be fine.' But nothing will be fine, because it's not just a matter of know-how and technology. Because to successfully export our environmental knowledge to India, you would also have to export the whole way society is organized." She was right about that, of course. But whereas others might hesitate over the implications of such ideas, she was not about to question the Greenpeace crusade. Her terms were unconditional: if she had her way, India would have to lose.

What Greenpeace wants from shipbreaking must seem in the tidy confines of Holland to be perfectly fair—essentially, to treat shipping as if it were any other orderly industry and to hold it responsible for its toxic by-products and the safety of its workers. The problem is that shipping is like the larger world in which it operates—an inherently disorderly affair, existing mostly beyond the reach of nations and their laws, beyond the dikes and coastal horizons, and out across the open seas. It is not exactly a criminal industry, but it is an amoral and stubbornly anarchic one. And it admits as much about itself. At the shipbreaking conference in Amsterdam in June 1999, one of the all-important London-based maritime insurers raised the fear that if somehow the reforms went through, even assuming that they applied only to the most visible European shippers, there would be a corresponding increase in mysterious sinkings.

But others in the business told me that the more likely effect of such reforms, as long as money can be made in Third World scrap, would simply be a new and less direct route to Asia: ships would pass through more hands, would maybe live longer plying faraway waters under new names and flags, and would still end up dying on some filthy beach. Already, there was evidence that some European shippers had begun to find new foreign buyers for vessels that they would normally have sold directly to scrappers, and Shell had decided to reinspect and retain certain aging tankers rather than face the wrath of Greenpeace again. Paradoxically, such policies may lead to an increase in hull failures and spills of the sort that have already soiled the once-pristine coasts of Portugal, France, and Spain. Greenpeace has protested the lax enforcement of European port controls to good effect—but the ocean, like the world, is terribly difficult to police.

Few observers seriously believe that as a result of Western pressures, South Asia as a whole will lose the scrapping business. But this offers little solace to the scrappers at Alang, because there is serious competition within the region, especially from Bangladesh. At Chittagong, starvation wages are paid, and labor and safety regulations are utterly lacking, so a shipbreaker can send a thousand barefoot men to tear apart a single vessel and scrap even a supertanker in six months. Bangladesh is not so much a nation as a condition of distress, and any attempt to regulate the industry there would obviously be futile. As a result of this commercial advantage, the Bangladeshis can pay top dollar for ships. During my stay at Alang, such international competition had forced the bidding level for scrap ships above the price necessary to break even within India, and the scrappers currently acquiring vessels were having to gamble on a significant rise in the Indian metal market. It was a dangerous time.

Pravin Nagarsheth was not sanguine about Alang's prospects. He worried that the Indian beach had been singled out for special criticism, and that the publicity of the Greenpeace campaign was exacerbating the existing competitive pressures. There was evidence, he said, that some of the biggest shippers had begun quietly to shy away from India entirely and to direct their ships to more discreet beaches. He worried also about the process within India whereby the European campaign seemed to be changing domestic attitudes toward Alang—a change that in the end may prove more threatening to the work there than the eventual enactment of foreign laws. Either way, Nagarsheth wanted me to know how little it would take to destroy Alang.

Jaysukh Bai, the boss of Plot 138, was a relief to me, because he seemed almost unaware that his work might be considered wrong. He was a simple man who knew the mechanics of the trade. As if I might not have heard, he said, "There are certain Western lobbies who are interested that shipbreaking not continue." But he never once mentioned any concern for safety or the environment. He never once mentioned his workers. He said, "I am worried about the future. What is important is the turnaround time. If there are too many rules to comply with, we will waste time." It was a statement of fact, hard to argue with. I asked him how many ships he had broken. He counted on his fingers, because he remembered every one. Eventually he answered: thirty-eight. He told me they included the biggest ship ever grounded at Alang, a French supertanker of fifty-two thousand tons. Those were the good old days. With that ship Captain Pandey must have had great fun.

The one here now, the old *Sun Ray* from the Maldives, was only fifteen thousand tons, but it seemed very big to me. Jaysukh Bai told me he could do the job on it, start to finish, in a mere four months. That was very fast, and he may have been bragging. But only one month into it, the superstructure and fuel tanks had been cut up and hauled away, and the lightened hull was being winched forward on the high tides and consumed with voracious efficiency. Even the birds joined in, pecking through the debris along the waterline, as alert as any man on the shore to the shreds of opportunity—a shard of torn plywood, pieces of wire for nest building, splinters of steel. I went down to the ship when I could, past the ground crews who by now had grown used to my presence. At the torn bow, I climbed through the broken bilge into the huge forward cargo hold, now open to the sky. The ship was mine to wander—up precarious ladders to the main deck high above, through passageways and equipment rooms where the peeling paint and rusted steel gave evidence of the years of wandering and hard use, and ultimately of neglect. Nonetheless, I felt a sort of awe, and was never in a hurry to leave. After climbing back down from the main deck into the hold, I sometimes walked deeper still into the depths of the ship. It was eerie and dim on the inside, an immense man-made cavern filled with hoarse warning cries, the hiss of torches, sparks, smoke, heavy hammering, the sound of falling debris. It had paths made of narrow beams with oil-slick footing, and sudden gaping holes that seemed to emerge out of nowhere. If you fell there, you could certainly die. But after the glare and heat outside, it was also pleasantly cool. The workers did not seem to mind my presence, or even to wonder about it. They appeared sometimes like ghosts, moving fast and in file without speaking. They were very dirty. They were very poor. But they lacked the look of death that I had seen on the men in the Bhavnagar rerolling mill. They were purposeful. Toward the stern, where sunlight streamed through rough-cut ventilation holes and struck the oil-blackened walls, the towering engine room had the Gothic beauty of a cathedral—a monument to the forces of a new world.

CPSIA information can be obtained
at www.ICGtesting.com
Printed in the USA
LVHW092256291121
704803LV00016B/305

9 780865 477223